Endowment Builder

Practical Ideas for Securing Endowment Gifts

SECOND EDITION

Scott C. Stevenson, Editor

WILEY

978-1-118-69311-7   ISBN

978-1-118-70428-8   ISBN (online)

Endowment Builder —
2nd Edition

Practical Ideas for
Securing Endowment Gifts

Published by

Stevenson, Inc.

P.O. Box 4528 • Sioux City, Iowa • 51104

Phone 712.239.3010 • Fax 712.239.2166

www.stevensoninc.com

TABLE OF CONTENTS

Endowment Builder: Practical Ideas for Securing Endowment Gifts, Second Edition.
Edited by Scott C. Stevenson.
© 2009 Stevenson, Inc. Published 2009 by Stevenson, Inc.

SET THE STAGE FOR BUILDING YOUR ENDOWMENT

Those nonprofit organizations that are serious about building their endowments take key steps to demonstrate the importance they place on endowment: creating an environment conducive to endowment investments, educating advancement staff, setting endowment goals and more.

To secure transformational gifts it is important to understand who makes such gifts, the motivation behind their gifts, the most effective solicitation tactics and the characteristics of one's organization to attract such gifts.

Create Philanthropic Culture to Attract Transformational Gifts

Transformational gifts go beyond major gifts in their unique capacity to impact an organization's programs, perception and future. But many nonprofits aren't doing all they could to land such gifts, say Sandra Ehrlich, director of fund development services, and Dawn M.S. Miller, senior consultant, Zielinski Companies (St. Louis, MO).

Organizational conditions and strategies that attract transformational gifts, say Ehrlich and Miller, include:

✓ Impact-oriented mission, core values and vision.

✓ Results-oriented, values-laden marketing and messages.

✓ Strong board, staff and volunteer leadership (In other words, donors believe in the people running the organization).

✓ Opportunity for impact and donor involvement.

✓ Commitment to building donor relationships and stewardship.

Potential transformational donors need to be part of the solution, says Miller: "As long-term investors, they are searching for opportunities to transform themselves, the organizations they support, the issues they are concerned about and the communities they care about."

Many transformational gifts are from the "new" philanthropists, the fundraising experts say: cyber and venture capital rich; women; ethnic and racial groups previously underrepresented in philanthropy; and those who have inherited wealth through the current American intergenerational transfer of several trillions of dollars.

"These investment-minded donors are drawn to institutions, programs and projects by their impact, issues, innovation and involvement," says Miller. "Therefore many of the 'old' methods of identifying, cultivating and even soliciting must be reevaluated from the 'new' philanthropists' perspective. Since many of the new philanthropists are less-experienced donors, they typically don't show up on the 'usual suspects' lists. To complicate matters, they often prefer to seek out organizations that fulfill their philanthropic dreams and aspirations."

She adds that many individuals capable of transformational gifts have formed their own philanthropic organizations through donor-advised funds within their venture capital or financial firms, independent family foundations or community foundations.

To attract a transformational gift, organizations must present a results-oriented face and focus on the gift's results, not organizational needs, they add.

"Focus on the issues, ideas and values inherent and embedded within the mission," says Ehrlich. "Typically, donor-centered solicitation of transformational gifts should be done through personal conversations and face-to-face contact with the donor and recipients whose lives will change or be transformed by the gift. However these are, in many cases, success-oriented, busy people, so you will need to adapt your systems and communication styles to meet their needs."

Seven Key Reasons Donors Make Transformational Gifts

Securing a transformational gift for your organization begins with understanding what motivates major donors.

Fundraising experts Sandra Ehrlich, director of fund development services, and Dawn M.S. Miller, senior consultant, Zielinski Companies (St. Louis, MO), cite seven reasons that donors make transformational gifts:

1. They believe in your organization's mission, core values and vision.

2. They believe in your organization's unique qualifications to provide programs and services, both now and in the future.

3. Their gift will change or save a life.

4. They want to make a difference in their community through your organization.

5. They believe your organization will use the funds effectively per their intent.

6. They want to join others in a valuable cause.

7. You asked them to make an investment in your organization and community.

Sources: Sandra G. Ehrlich, Director of Fund Development Services, and Dawn M.S. Miller, Senior Consultant, Zielinski Companies, St. Louis, MO. Phone (800) 489-2150; (314) 644-2150. E-mail: sehrlich@zielinskico.com or dmiller@zielinskico.com

SET THE STAGE FOR BUILDING YOUR ENDOWMENT

Undergo Development Audit Before Launching Major Fundraising Effort

Audit Proves Valuable For One Nonprofit

When officials with Hand-in-Paw, Inc. (Birmingham, AL) began planning a capital campaign, they turned to The Development Group (Birmingham, AL) to conduct a development audit.

Beth Franklin, executive director, Hand-in-Paw, says the audit took about six months and included meetings with herself, the associate director and other key staff to gather information before surveying board members on their commitment and views of organizational capacity.

Items evaluated in the audit included: bylaws; articles of incorporation; strategic plan; organizational charts; database; software; fund development policies/procedures; fund development successes; marketing and published pieces; annual report; gift acceptance; gift acknowledgement; and case statement.

After the interviews and internal document evaluation, Franklin says, the consultants presented the findings to the executive committee, governance committee and herself.

Results from the audit included:

✓ A validation of the strong network and engagement of stakeholders in the nonprofit's mission.

✓ A reiteration of the need to have strong infrastructure through systems, staffing and volunteer engagement.

✓ Reminder of the critical role that strategic direction has on current and future fundraising goals.

✓ The critical role a solid donor database plays in a good development program and that it must be able to function efficiently.

Source: Beth Franklin, Executive Director, Hand-in-Paw, Inc., Birmingham, AL. Phone (205) 322-5144. E-mail: info@handinpaw.org

If you would like to increase philanthropic gifts or are preparing for a capital campaign, a development audit is considered the best preparation for these activities.

The development audit or internal assessment is an opportunity to review internal corporate documents, staff skills, fundraising procedures/outcomes and organizational effectiveness before proceeding with fund development planning or a capital campaign.

Barbara Shelton, president, The Development Group (Birmingham, AL), outlines typical steps taken during a development process that covers the nonprofit's development practices and reflects its uniqueness:

1. **Select outside counsel to conduct development audit.** Shelton recommends interviewing consultants with a track record in the process who can provide references.

2. **Preparation phase.** Consultants meet with organization's leaders to create and outline a footprint for the audit and materials needed for review. Nonprofit leaders share goals for the audit and greatest opportunities or challenges they may be experiencing in fundraising, staffing or board involvement. Leaders may be asked to evaluate themselves in a written survey and in-person meeting that may include ranking perception of the organization among stakeholders, evaluating their own effectiveness in fundraising for the organization and rating effectiveness of fundraising activities.

3. **Review four areas: organizational, development/fundraising, communications and volunteer.** Shelton says each item may be reviewed on or off site.

   ❑ **Organizational** — Corporate documents, strategic plan, policies, overall fund development plan, board list, affiliations and case statement, staff and internal items.

   ❑ **Development/Fundraising** — Annual plans; staff plan; fundraising activities and outcomes; grant requests; donor recognition and acknowledgement plan and activities; donor database; gift processing and procedures; staff systems; fundraising appeals; campaign history; internal conditions that influenced fundraising outcomes.

   ❑ **Communications** — All fundraising print, electronic and PR activities.

   ❑ **Volunteer** — The organization's volunteer fundraising structure.

Shelton says cost of a development audit can range from $5,000 to $20,000-plus and depend on factors such as geographic region, organization size and depth of audit needed.

Source: Barbara Shelton, President, The Development Group, Birmingham, AL. Phone (205) 422-5147. E-mail: barbshelton@charter.net

Benefits of a Development Audit

Barbara Shelton, president, The Development Group (Birmingham, AL), answers questions about the importance of a development audit:

Why is it important for nonprofits to conduct a development audit?

"It gets the organizational house in order so when activity increases and more dollars are realized, the organization is ready. The audit puts everyone (board, staff and volunteers) on the same page and helps set priorities. It ensures proper stewardship. And it creates good infrastructure and systems, which is good management."

What can be determined from a development audit that can save a nonprofit problems in a capital campaign?

- "Knowing areas of strength and weakness prepares an organization for the natural flow of a campaign.

- "Procedures are put in place for gift processing and acceptance.

- "Campaign fundraising will work better alongside annual fundraising activities.

- "Taking time to plan and think through all possibilities that could come up in a campaign is just good business and helps the nonprofit respond quickly to opportunities.

- "Capital campaign fundraising is not an event, it is a process. Carefully planned and executed, a campaign will bring energy and life to the nonprofit."

SET THE STAGE FOR BUILDING YOUR ENDOWMENT

Establish Yearly Endowment Goals

Outline yearly endowment goals to begin to make headway in marketing and building your endowment.

Most advancement offices establish a yearly operational plan that includes plans on how to generate and meet unrestricted annual gift goals. Far fewer, however, establish goals and objectives tied to generating endowment gifts.

You need not be in the midst of a capital campaign to work at generating gifts of endowment, and that job should not be the sole responsibility of a planned gifts officer. Outright gifts can be made as well.

Although the realization of larger endowment gifts often takes longer than one year to matriculate, a proactive plan will begin the "pipeline" process that makes such gifts eventual realities.

Here are some examples of yearly quantifiable endowment objectives:

- To solicit X number of prospects for endowment pledges.

- To develop/submit X corporate and/or foundation proposals asking for endowment grants.

- To coordinate a special event, proceeds from which will be directed to the endowment.

- To identify and cultivate no less than X prospects toward the realization of endowment commitments.

Advice on Setting Endowment Objectives

In establishing yearly or multi-year endowment objectives, be sure to include the goal of inviting donors who have already established named endowment funds to add to the funds.

It's easy to think in terms of going after new donors to establish new named funds. However, it's equally important to continually invite those who have already established funds to add to them, either through outright gifts, planned gifts or both.

And, quite frankly, it should be easier to convince existing donors to add to existing endowment funds than to find new donors. After all, those donors have already demonstrated their belief in your cause and the importance of endowment.

Create an Image Worthy of Major Gift Support

Determine whether your organization projects an image worthy of endowment gifts.

To attract sizeable gifts, your organization must be perceived as worthy of such gifts. Institutions with a history of ongoing major gift support share the following characteristics:

- Successive years of balanced budgets.

- An adequate operating reserve.

- A CEO who has vision and surrounds him/herself with an accomplished team of managers.

- Well-maintained facilities.

- A board of trustees made up of persons who are financially capable, highly supportive and accomplished in their fields.

- Regular publicity that addresses the organization's accomplishments.

- An annual report that honestly speaks to the financial well-being of the institution.

- Highly satisfied clients (those served by your organization).

- A growing endowment.

- Successful programs addressing the institution's mission.

While this list may not be complete, it sets the stage for an image that attracts big gifts.

Rule of Thumb

- Most highly skilled development professionals can manage 600 to 800 cultivation moves per year. Knowing this, plan and schedule specific moves six to 12 months in advance to achieve the greatest efficiency in how you use your available time and your precious financial resources.

Set Yearly Endowment Goals

If it's your intent to grow your endowment, then you should have yearly goals in place aimed at doing just that. And if you're just getting started, set goals that are challenging but realistic. For example, one of your endowment goals may be "to secure no fewer than 10 $10,000 or more named endowment commitments."

SET THE STAGE FOR BUILDING YOUR ENDOWMENT

How to Prepare for an Endowment-only Campaign

While capital and endowment campaigns have many similarities, they also have differences — most notably in the case for support, opportunities for recognition and how funds are used — says Jennifer Furla, executive vice president, Jeffrey Byrne & Associates (Kansas City, MO). Knowing those differences can help guarantee the success of an endowment-only campaign.

One major difference? "Unlike capital campaigns that have highly defined timelines that underlie their case for support and may involve bridge financing to accomplish their goal," Furla says, "endowment campaigns usually can take a longer view."

Furla, who is also on the board of the Giving USA Foundation (Glenview, IL), says that compared to capital campaigns, endowment-only campaigns:

- **Allow for more flexibility** in accepting, counting and recording gifts.

- **See planned gifts as more appropriate for and playing a larger role.**

- **Offer more deferred giving opportunities** (although they can be seeded/funded with current gifts in a prescribed campaign format). Organizations should have an existing planned giving promotion program in place and know which donors have already included the organization in estate plans.

- **Require a more thorough examination of internal readiness.** In addition to written gift policy and procedures, organizations need an endowment structure in place — not a board-restricted fund — before launching an endowment campaign. A gift policy should include all types of gifts, including deferred giving opportunities and detailing how the organization intends to spend the endowment.

- **Require extensive donor research and cultivation.** Prospect research companies such as Blackbaud and Magic give wealth- and asset-based overlays and even indicate where donors are giving to similar causes. Endowment donors are your best, top donors who have been with you a long time and give consistently. An endowment campaign typically is not the type of campaign to be in acquisition mode.

A feasibility study is as important for an endowment campaign as it is for a capital campaign, says Furla: "The feasibility study will allow you to refine your case for support and determine your direction, cultivate top donors and learn which donors have already provided for your organization in their estate plans."

When considering an endowment campaign, she advises, one of your first steps should be a highly focused board discussion on how your cause's goals relate to your strategic planning, and what the endowment campaign will and won't produce.

A key question to pose to board members: "Is an endowment campaign even appropriate for our organization?" "Some institutions and corporate donors will not give to endowment," Furla says. "Research also shows that post-baby boomer generations are less likely to give to endowment because they want to be more active in their giving and have greater control over the investment of their dollars."

Other steps to take before launching an endowment campaign, Furla says, include:

- Conducting a thorough assessment of your donor database to determine how many additional prospects you will need to support an endowment campaign.

- Orchestrating a feasibility study and testing it within your own constituency, with your top leadership and with the broader community.

- Making sure all members of your board understand that while an endowment campaign is not a capital building project, they, as board members, are still expected to lead the campaign with their own gifts.

- Realizing an endowment campaign is a longer decision-making period for donors, so the campaign may have a longer fundraising timeline than a capital campaign.

A first step to ensuring a successful endowment-only campaign is to understand how it differs from a capital campaign.

Source: Jennifer Furla, Executive Vice President, Jeffrey Byrne & Associates, Kansas City, MO. Phone (800) 222-9233. E-mail: jfurla@fundraisingjba.com

SET THE STAGE FOR BUILDING YOUR ENDOWMENT

Endowment Committee Brings Focus

Whether you are about to establish an endowment committee of existing donors, board members and/or others, or are looking to fine-tune responsibilities of an existing group, an active endowment committee can significantly help raise endowment gifts.

Challenge your endowment committee or endowment advisory group to:

No endowment committee? It's a great way to bring focus to raising gifts for your endowment.

- Develop an endowment acceptance policy.
- Identify endowment gift opportunities.
- Offer formal input regarding the creation of endowment marketing materials.
- Establish named endowment funds of their own.
- Review and contribute to a quarterly newsletter that addresses endowment topics.
- Make cultivation and solicitation calls on prospects.
- Establish stewardship strategies to recognize those who give endowment gifts.
- Establish or provide input for an endowment investment policy.
- Identify strategies promoting endowment among agents of wealth: attorneys, trust officers, CPAs and others.
- Act as a steering committee for an endowment-only campaign.

Learn the Psychology Behind Endowment Giving

If part of your job includes encouraging others to establish named endowment funds, there's a great way to learn more about the psychology behind such giving: Establish an endowment gift of your own.

Creating an endowment fund of your own will open your eyes to the motivation behind endowment giving.

To begin, you know better than most that nearly anyone, even those of modest means, can establish an endowed fund. (Use $10,000 as the minimum amount required over time.) You can purchase a life insurance policy and name the charity as owner and beneficiary. Or, you can make monthly or quarterly payroll deductions as a way to build your endowed fund over a period of years. Or, you can establish an endowed fund through a combination of outright and planned gifts.

Here's the point: The best way to understand the psychology of endowment giving is to start a fund of your own. You will find yourself looking at the entire gift-giving process — particularly as it relates to endowment giving — in a more informed light. You will find the experience to be both energizing and highly gratifying. The sales psychology you use to encourage others to establish or add to endowment funds will be based, in part, on your own experience as a donor. Plus, you will be in a much better position to invite others to give as well by telling them that you have already established a fund.

Use Mind Mapping to Brainstorm Fundraising Strategies

Have you ever used mind mapping to strategize fundraising approaches?

According to Wikipedia, a mind map is "a diagram used to represent words, ideas, tasks or other items linked to a central key word or idea..... it encourages a brainstorming approach to any given organizational task."

Although there are online tools that can be helpful for mind mapping, you can just as easily begin with a topic written on a piece of paper. Place a circle around it and branch out from there with ideas. Visualizing concepts and characteristics will lead you to next steps.

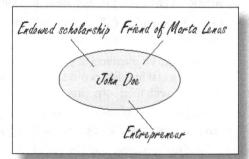

SET THE STAGE FOR BUILDING YOUR ENDOWMENT

The ABCs of Endowments

It's ironic: Many major gifts officers who may be perfectly at ease talking multimillion-dollar gifts with donors or carrying donors' five-figure checks in their wallets are at the same time hesitant when it comes to promoting endowment gifts.

That needn't be the case.

Creating an endowment can take anywhere from a single meeting to months to complete. It all depends on donor intent, gift size and size of your organization. It will involve the donor, major gifts officer, treasurer, legal representation, stewardship personnel and, if the gift is to involve retirement or estate funds, a certified financial planner.

Determining and honoring a donor's intent is the most important aspect of creating an endowment.

Once a donor agrees that an endowment is his/her gift vehicle of choice, the major gifts officer must outline the organization's investment policies and rules for distributing income. Next — and of utmost importance — development staff must precisely capture the donor's intent for how endowment proceeds will be spent. This is the heart of the endowment creation process.

Donor intent can be recorded in a predesigned endowment agreement form that allows a major gifts officer to enter investment and distribution information before meeting with the donor and to fill in donor information later.

Depending on a nonprofit's size, the number of personnel who must review the endowment agreement varies. In addition to the treasurer, it may require signatures from multiple personnel, depending on who will be affected by the implementation of this agreement.

Once all interested parties agree that the future endowment is legitimate, the major gifts officer should prepare two copies of a formal endowment agreement, being sure to honor the donor's original wishes as closely as possible.

The organization's representatives should sign both copies before it is presented to the donor to sign. This is extremely important, as the donor's signature should represent the final step in the creation process.

The donor should be allowed to keep one of the originals, and the other should be filed with the organization.

The procedure for marketing endowment gifts is really not all that different from promoting other types of major gifts.

Endowment Comparison Helps to Build the Case for Support

If you're attempting to generate more endowment gifts for your charity, it never hurts to compare yourself to the competition — or to those charities to which you aspire.

Seeing how your organization's endowment size compares to that of other charities helps prospects understand endowment's importance. You have nothing to lose and everything to gain by comparing your organization to those whose endowments are far larger. Prospects may respond:

- Why isn't our endowment equal in size to theirs?
- Why should we be the poor kid on the block? We need the resources just as much as those organizations do.
- Just imagine what we could accomplish if we had an endowment equal in size to these organizations!

The act of getting a response from your prospects — whatever it is — helps to get them thinking and make them more aware of the need for endowment support.

Earmark Proceeds for Endowment

If you're just starting to build an endowment fund or you find it particularly challenging to generate endowment gifts, consider starting to funnel designated proceeds to your endowment. Here are some examples that could be board approved as designated for endowment:

- Revenue from an annual special event.

- Project revenue — calendar, cookbook, holiday ornament or other types of fundraising sales.

- Unrestricted bequests — Many nonprofits have a policy in place that automatically directs unrestricted bequests to their endowments.

- Gifts from one or more particular groups (e.g., board member contributions, gifts from religious institutions).

- Year-end revenue that may exceed what was budgeted. (It does happen!)

SET THE STAGE FOR BUILDING YOUR ENDOWMENT

> Content not available in this edition

Endowment Comparisons Help Rally the Troops

Have you ever compared your endowment with similar organizations whose endowments are substantially larger than yours as a way to encourage greater constituent support?

Elon University (Elon, NC) officials have used benchmarking with other institutions as a way to raise the sights of those close to Elon, according to Chuck Davis, senior director of individual giving. The bar graph Elon officials prepared helps illustrate how Elon's endowment is lacking when compared to similar institutions.

Davis shares his thoughts about the value of comparing endowments:

> Content not available in this edition

Encourage support of your organization's endowment by comparing it to similar organizations whose endowments are substantially larger.

Why does it make sense to compare your endowment to others' endowments?

"Part of it is cultural. Elon, specifically, has a long tradition of trying to be a best practices type of institution and we naturally compare ourselves to other institutions, both regionally and nationally, on a lot of different fronts. I think it's also for our constituency groups that have seen Elon rise at a phenomenal rate over the last 10 to 15 years. It has been motivating, I think, for a lot of them to see that we're competing with a completely different set of peer institutions. When we compare ourselves to other institutions on the endowment front, we see that we lag behind and it motivates people to want to be better."

How do you use those comparisons to build your own endowment?

"We put them in bar graph form in our case statements, which we have completed for use in our feasibility study for our next campaign. We use it. The president uses it. It is eye-opening. It educates our external constituents who think we are wealthy because of our beautiful campus and exceptional facilities. The best way to communicate that we are not is to show them peer institutions they are used to and seeing that we are very low in endowment. I think it's motivating for our constituency groups to want to better that benchmark."

Do you have any proof that making the comparison is paying off?

"Our president was in a leadership briefing with a diverse group of alumni, friends and parents. After that meeting, an older alumnus came up to the president and said, 'I had no idea (the endowment was so low) and I am completely ashamed and feel that it is my responsibility to help change that for Elon.' We have put it out there and we're beginning to see people understand better what an endowment is and they are responding with larger gifts than we have gotten in the endowment before."

Source: Charles E. "Chuck" Davis III, Senior Director of Individual Giving, Elon University, Elon, NC. Phone (336) 278-7443. E-mail: cdavis11@elon.edu

Endowment Ideas for Beginners

If your organization has little history of receiving endowment gifts, consider having your board approve a policy statement similar to this:

"All undesignated gifts of $5,000 or more will be automatically restricted to [Name of Organization]'s endowment fund."

This ensures that such windfalls are not used to fund immediate needs.

Endowment Builder: Practical Ideas for Securing Endowment Gifts, Second Edition.
Edited by Scott C. Stevenson.
© 2009 Stevenson, Inc. Published 2009 by Stevenson, Inc.

AWARENESS BUILDING AND EDUCATION MEASURES

Once the internal stage is set to build an endowment, ongoing public education is critical. Before one can begin to seek endowment gifts, constituents need to be aware of what an endowment is and the enormous role it can play in the charity's future. It's not enough to have an awareness-building campaign; the educational and information-sharing process should be continual.

Five Ways to Publicize Your Endowment

People are more likely to support your endowment if the topic is an ongoing part of their conscious. That's why it's important to come up with ways to keep the subject before them.

To increase endowment awareness and accompanying gift opportunities:

1. Throw a celebration when your endowment hits a milestone year: tops a certain dollar amount; has been in existence for so many years; etc.

2. Regularly profile in your newsletter or magazine a particular named endowment fund: the name behind the fund; the impact it has had and continues to have on those you serve; and more.

3. Create a club or society with special benefits for all who contribute to your endowment — those who contribute a minimum amount during the past fiscal year and/or those who establish naming endowment gifts.

4. Formalize a yearlong calendar of strategies and events bringing attention to endowment opportunities.

5. Seek donors' approval to publicize their endowment gifts whenever they occur.

Increase public awareness of your endowment by using several marketing tactics to keep it in front of your constituents' faces.

Offer Endowment FAQs on Your Website

Since many people are less familiar with endowments and how they work, it makes good sense to include frequently asked questions (FAQs) that address endowment topics on your website.

Common endowment questions you might want to pose and answer include:

✓ What is an endowment?
✓ What's a named endowment?
✓ Why establish an endowment?
✓ What is the minimum amount necessary to establish a named endowment?
✓ What endowment funding opportunities are available?
✓ How is an endowed fund invested?
✓ Who oversees or manages the endowment?
✓ What is the current value of the endowment?
✓ What named funds currently exist and how are they used?
✓ Can I establish a named endowment fund over time?
✓ Can I add to an endowed fund after my lifetime?
✓ How do I go about starting a named endowment fund?

Before Raising Your Endowment Minimum....

What's the minimum gift amount required to establish a named endowment fund at your organization? $10,000? $25,000? $100,000?

Before you decide to raise your minimum requirement, be sure to widely publicize that it is going up. Give yourself up to a year after making the announcement. Why? You can use that time window as a great marketing opportunity: Establish your named endowment now, before prices go up!

This sales method — the deal/concession closing — gives prospects the impression they're making a smart choice by making a gift now.

Include Key Information In Endowment Brochure

If you are actively marketing endowment gifts, you no doubt have a booklet or brochure that addresses endowment gift opportunities. Besides a list of available naming endowment opportunities, what other useful information does the publication include?

Here's some of what you might include in your endowment handout:

- Historical account of your endowment — when it was started and why.
- Investment philosophy and average rate of return.
- Biographies on investment committee board members.
- Profile on investment management company.
- Endowment growth chart.
- Anecdotes of how endowment funds have impacted your organization and those you serve.
- Descriptions of ways to make endowment gifts (e.g., planned gift descriptions, outright gifts using various types of assets, etc.).
- How particular types of endowment gifts can benefit the donor(s).

AWARENESS BUILDING AND EDUCATION MEASURES

Make Endowment-building Initiatives Obvious

How proactive are you in making the public aware of your intent to build an endowment? Sometimes, even charities with well-established endowments don't do enough to keep endowment opportunities in the eyes of the public.

Here are some practical examples of how you can continually keep the public aware of plans to build your endowment:

1. Regularly meet with agents of wealth — attorneys, accountants, trust officers, insurance agents and others. These professionals come in contact with those who might have a desire to make large charitable gifts.

2. Include endowment facts and figures in your annual report and other print communications. Help your constituency become more aware of where your endowment presently stands, where you would like it to be and why.

3. Make use of every opportunity to publicize those who are making gifts — both planned and outright — to your endowment. Have a planned gifts club in place.

4. Establish an endowment committee to help promote endowment gifts and monitor progress.

If Your Endowment Is Growing, Tout It!

Is your endowment growing? If so, use a graph to publicize its success to your donors and community through local newspapers, your external newsletter and annual report.

Those who give to an endowment like knowing they are giving to a winner. So if your endowment is growing, let your donors and supporters know.

Will donors lessen or stop their giving if they see a growing endowment? No way! Your good stewardship of their gifts will only encourage increased support.

Include a graph such as the example shown here in your newsletter, annual report, letter to major donors and other publications to illustrate the growth taking place in your organization's endowment.

Haggar Art Center Endowment Growth

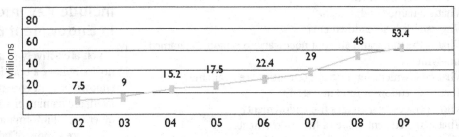

Be Proactive in Addressing Endowment Issues

If your endowment has been negatively impacted by the economy don't be hesitant to confront the issue head on with donors. It will gain you respect with them knowing you are willing to share even bad news.

Has your nonprofit's endowment been negatively impacted by the economy?

Rather than waiting for donors and would-be donors to ask questions, update your constituency on current endowment issues. Prepare to honestly answer their questions.

What might people ask? Here's a sampling of questions:

• Where does the endowment stand presently?

• How has your endowment been impacted by the economy?

• How will the current economic downturn impact the named fund we have established?

• How are the endowment funds presently invested, and what changes either have taken place or will take place with regard to investment strategies?

• What safeguards do you have in place should the economy worsen?

AWARENESS BUILDING AND EDUCATION MEASURES

Identify and Prioritize All Endowment Gift Opportunities

Whether you have a substantial endowment in place or you're just getting started in establishing one, it's important to identify fundable endowment opportunities and prioritize their importance to your organization.

As much as you may need unrestricted endowment gifts, which generate annual interest to underwrite yearly general operations, many donors prefer to earmark their investments to projects that can make a noticeable and visible difference.

As you gear up to market restricted endowment opportunities, follow this process:

1. **Establish endowment parameters.** At what level, for instance, can a donor have the choice of establishing a named fund? What's the maximum number of years donors will have to pay out endowment pledges? To what degree will you allow donors to spell out endowment restrictions?

2. **Identify all endowment possibilities.** If you have existing restricted endowment accounts, list those first. Then, review your organization's budget, first by category, then by line item. What categories and line items within your existing budget could be endowed?

3. **Prioritize each identified endowment possibility based on two factors:** 1) its importance to fulfilling your organization's needs and mission; 2) its fundability — its attractiveness to potential donors. After going through this process, you may decide that some potential endowment projects should be deleted or tabled.

As you go through the final step, consider inviting small groups or individual potential donors to review your draft list and offer their opinions. Why? The act of engaging them in the process at this point will help them to buy into investing in endowment. Plus, their responses will provide clues as to their funding interests.

Your final list of restricted endowment opportunities can be incorporated into marketing materials. In doing so, be sure that unrestricted endowment gifts top your invitation to invest.

It's important to identify fundable endowment opportunities and prioritize their importance.

Sample restricted endowment opportunities.

RESTRICTED ENDOWMENT OPPORTUNITIES
ABC ART CENTER

ENDOWMENT OPPORTUNITY	GIFT MINIMUMS
Executive Director Fund — Gifts directed to this fund will underwrite the salary and benefits of the executive director position, allowing us to attract the most capable individual the nation has to offer.	$1 million
Lecture Series — Fund will be used to underwrite an annual lecture series devoted to various aspects of arts topics.	$250,000
Acquisition Fund — Annual interest used to purchase works for our permanent collection.	$100,000
Youth Education/Programs Fund — Annual interest from this fund will allow art center staff to ensure the future of arts programs and education relating to our region's youth. The size of the fund will determine the scope of new and expanded offerings.	$100,000
Annual Juried Artists' Exhibition — This fund will underwrite our annual juried artists' exhibition and allow us to expand it further.	$50,000
Exhibit Fund — Yearly proceeds underwrite cost of bringing exhibits to our facility.	$50,000
Gift Shop Fund — Yearly income will underwrite costs associated with the gift shop and enable us to enhance marketing efforts and retail opportunities for area artists' works.	$50,000
Art Maintenance and Restoration Fund — Proceeds used to maintain and restore artwork within our permanent collection.	$25,000
Docents Program — Annual interest underwrites costs associated with existing docents program and allows further expansion of program.	$25,000
Emerging Artists' Fund — Proceeds allow the art center to encourage and nurture budding artists within a 100-mile radius of the art center.	$25,000

AWARENESS BUILDING AND EDUCATION MEASURES

Explain Endowments' Many Benefits in Simple Terms

A simple one-page letter can be an effective way to market the benefits an endowment offers.

Endowed funds mean security, sustainability and power for your organization. Unfortunately, most donors do not understand those benefits and are apprehensive about contributing to something they cannot see or feel (buildings, equipment, etc.).

An excellent way to address this problem is to create a simple, one-page explanation of the incredible benefits that endowments provide. Explain that endowments are perpetual and their ultimate benefit is the fact that they can last for decades while contributing regular income to your organization. They are, quite literally, "the gift that keeps on giving."

You'll find that most prospects and donors, upon understanding the true value of an endowed fund, will be excited about the opportunity.

Anecdotes, Stats Show Endowment Gift's Impact

Offer prospects an assortment of ideas to show how a gift to your endowment fund can make a difference in the lives of those you serve.

When you look at a mature tree, what runs through your mind?

Some might simply take in its beauty. Others might think of the shade it provides. Still others may ponder its age, who planted it and the many seasons it has weathered.

We all perceive the world differently. It's the same with endowment gifts. While one person may be in awe of having an endowment in his/her name, another may be impressed by its continuing longevity. Still others may be struck by the number of people the fund helps.

As you market named endowment opportunities, be prepared to use an assortment of anecdotes and descriptions to explain the significance of such gifts (see suggestions, left).

For additional ideas, meet with colleagues — perhaps even past endowment donors — to develop a menu of persuasive pitches you can use to convince prospects of the many values of giving named endowment funds.

Ways for Volunteers, Others To Explain a Gift's Value

✓ With this annual interest from such a scholarship fund, you could assist as many as eight students each year — that's 80 future leaders you would be helping over the next decade.

✓ Buildings come and go; but an endowment fund will continue to benefit those we serve for generations to come.

✓ By establishing a children's endowment fund for $250,000, you would bring hope into the lives of the youngsters who come to our facility.

✓ Creating an endowment fund in honor of your parents — while they are still alive and healthy — would be an awesome tribute.

Move Your Donors With a 'What If' Story

Inspire donors and would-be donors to give to your endowment by writing a 'what if' article for your organization's magazine or newsletter.

Once upon a time there was a community food bank stocked to the rafters with more than enough food to fill the empty stomachs of the community's hungry. Never again would the staff have to send a needy family away empty-handed. In fact, the food bank even began offering hot, nutritious meals daily in a warm, bright community room filled with laughter....

Part of your success in generating major gifts depends on your ability to inspire people to invest in your cause. One way to do so is through your newsletter or magazine.

As you consider article ideas for your primary communications tool, explore doing a "what if" article that visualizes what your organization would look like and what it could accomplish if you were to receive a transformational multimillion-dollar gift.

Your story might begin with "once upon a time" and then unfold with a portrait of the tremendous good your organization could to accomplish with fantastic facilities, state-of-the-art equipment, the most talented employees that money can hire and an endowment that rivals that of America's most well-known institutions.

Conclude your article with an uplifting invitation to help make the story a reality. Help the reader understand that the vision is within reach, but not without sacrifice.

AWARENESS BUILDING AND EDUCATION MEASURES

Characteristics of an Endowment Campaign

Although a capital campaign generally includes bricks and mortar projects, many often include an endowment component as well. Endowment-only campaigns are more rare but beginning to increase in popularity.

Although the effort to raise endowment funds should be ongoing — with no end date in sight — launching a more visible endowment campaign can produce greater momentum among potential donors and result in an acceleration of giving for this purpose.

If you're considering an endowment campaign, here are some characteristics of which you should be aware:

1. Endowment campaigns tend to realize greater success with older, more established nonprofits as compared to newer ones.

2. Endowment campaigns are more difficult to pull off when an organization's current finances are less stable.

3. Successful endowment campaigns help to ensure an organization's future and can tend to lessen the dependence on annual gift support.

4. *Donor benefit:* Endowment campaigns offer many attractive naming opportunities and, unlike a named building which may not always be around, a named endowment fund should continue on indefinitely, offering the donor greater immortality.

5. *Donor benefit:* Endowment gifts can be made during and after a donor's lifetime.

> *Although endowment-only campaigns are not as popular as capital campaigns — which may include both bricks and mortar and endowment — this sort of focused effort is becoming increasingly popular.*

Don't Become Too Dependent On Government Support

If your nonprofit organization is highly dependent on government support for its very existence, you have a great reason to be promoting gifts to your endowment.

Although some might argue that tax-supported agencies are already getting support — "so why should I contribute?" — it's your job to illustrate the exact opposite: "You have an opportunity to make us less government dependent, to ensure our needed services for generations to come."

Incorporate these messages into your justification of building an endowment that will reduce your dependency on government dollars:

- It's important that the government not dictate the kinds of services we provide or who can and cannot receive them.

- The needs of those we serve are always at a high level regardless of fluctuations in government appropriations.

- A respectable endowment will allow us to thrive; government dependency, at best, allows us to survive.

- The less time we have to spend lobbying for government support and completing reports, the more time we have available to fulfill our mission.

- It's not our job to become involved in politics, but rather to serve those in need.

- If more of our nation's nonprofit organizations could become less dependent on government funding, imagine how that would positively impact the taxpayers.

Include Endowment Info In Your Annual Report

To bring the importance of a growing endowment to your constituents' attention, devote one or two pages of your annual report (or honor roll of contributors) to that topic.

Include endowment information such as:

- Stats regarding the past year's endowment performance.

- Stats regarding the composition of endowment investments.

- A list of all named funds (and who contributed in the last fiscal year).

- Names of investment committee members and/or the firm that manages your endowment portfolio.

- A wish list of unfunded endowment opportunities.

- Future plans or hopes regarding your endowment and its impact on your organization.

- A summary of how someone can start a named endowment fund.

- Brief profiles of some of your endowment funds, who funded them and how they positively impact your organization and those you serve.

Endowment Builder: Practical Ideas for Securing Endowment Gifts, Second Edition.
Edited by Scott C. Stevenson.
© 2009 Stevenson, Inc. Published 2009 by Stevenson, Inc.

IDENTIFY ENDOWMENT FUNDING OPPORTUNITIES

This chapter shares a variety of endowment funding options you may wish to share with would-be donors, depending on the type of nonprofit organization you represent. The funding opportunities you present should be based on achieving balance between your needs and donors' funding interests.

How About Promoting Endowed Internships?

Endowed internships need not be for educational institutions only. They would make sense for any type of nonprofit that can benefit from interns.

If internships are prevalent in your organization, look to match donors with the educational opportunities and create endowed internships.

To honor the memory of her mother, Meredith Berkman and her husband Daniel Mintz made a $100,000 gift to Brandeis University (Waltham, MA) in 2008 to establish the Judith Cossin Berkman '59 Endowed Internship in Social Work.

Made in the 50th reunion year of Judith Cossin Berkman's graduating class, the gift will provide one Brandeis student pursuing a career in social work with a $5,000 stipend each summer. The university president, Jehuda Reinharz, traveled to New York to thank Meredith Berkman personally. The internship recipient also sent Berkman a thank-you. And the donor plans to attend her mother's 50th reunion and meet the first internship recipient.

Learn More on Endowed Internships

- The Judith Cossin Berkman '59 Endowed Internship in Social Work at www.brandeis.edu/hiatt/students/funding/wow/socialwork.html

- The Louis D. Brandeis Legacy Fund for Social Justice WOW Fellowship at www.brandeis.edu/hiatt/students/funding/wow/socialjustice.html

- The Eli J. Segal Citizen Service Fellowship at www.segalprogram.org

"When we get a gift like this, we steward it," says Nancy Winship, senior vice president of institutional advancement. "We try to build a relationship between the intern and the donor. We want donors who give these types of gifts to know that they are not writing a check blindly, but that their gift is going to students."

The Berkman Endowed Internship in Social Work is one of several internship programs in Brandeis' World of Work (WOW) Internship Funding Program. Another is the Louis D. Brandeis Legacy Fund for Social Justice WOW Fellowship, which supports undergraduate students performing an unpaid, full-time summer internship in an organization whose mission addresses issues of social justice. Stipends range from $3,500 to $4,000.

The Louis D. Brandeis Legacy Fund for Social Justice supports these awards and a wide range of activities that reflect the university's and Louis Brandeis' commitment to social justice. The legacy fund was established in 2006 by an anonymous alumni donor who stays in close contact with students he has helped through internships and scholarships.

Another internship program, the Eli J. Segal Citizen Service Fellowship, provides stipends to Brandeis undergraduate students in their sophomore or junior year, and graduate students at the university's Heller School for Social Policy and Management. Seven students — five undergraduate and two graduate — will serve internships this summer at government and nonprofit agencies based in Boston, New York and Washington, DC. As part of the program, former President Bill Clinton delivered the inaugural Segal Lecture in December 2007. The two were close friends before Segal's death in 2006.

"Donors of internship gifts feel that they will have a positive impact on a student's career," says Winship. "These donors tend to want to be more hands-on. The goal is to get them to do a few internships and then eventually a scholarship. It is just one step in building a relationship between them and our institution."

Source: Nancy Winship, Senior Vice President of Institutional Advancement, Brandeis University, Development & Alumni Relations, Waltham, MA. Phone (781) 736-4002. E-mail: winship@brandeis.edu

IDENTIFY ENDOWMENT FUNDING OPPORTUNITIES

Suggest Named Endowments Focusing on Outreach

If your services go beyond the community in which your organization resides, what are you doing to encourage major gifts from those geographically distant individuals and businesses?

People like giving at home, so why not establish endowment gift opportunities that allow donors to do that while still benefiting your nonprofit?

Explore offering named endowment gifts that address your nonprofit's outreach efforts. If, for instance, you represent a college or university with satellite campuses, offer named scholarships that benefit students attending a branch location. Or if your hospital provides services to neighboring communities, offer endowment gift opportunities that benefit the residents of those communities.

> ### Endowment Outreach Ideas
>
> Looking for endowment gift opportunities that benefit people outside of your immediate community?
>
> Here's a sampling of ideas:
>
> ✓ Scholarships for branch campus students.
>
> ✓ A traveling exhibit program.
>
> ✓ The purchase and maintenance of a mobile unit that visits neighboring communities.
>
> ✓ A facility maintenance or landscaping fund for satellite locations.
>
> ✓ An equipment acquisition fund.

Explore offering named endowment opportunities that address your organization's outreach efforts.

Why Not Endow Your Volunteer Recognition Program?

If your nonprofit relies heavily on volunteer involvement, why not seek one or more endowment gifts to fund your volunteer program? For starters, you could endow your annual volunteer recognition program.

Whether you currently host a volunteer recognition program or not, consider funding this worthwhile event with an endowment. Questions to ask in considering this new funding venture include:

- How much is needed to endow the entire recognition program as it now exists?

- With additional funds, how could we enhance the recognition program?

- Could we attract even more publicity (translation: possibility of new gifts and volunteers) if we were able to give our volunteer recognition efforts greater visibility?

Identify one or more donors who believe in the value of volunteer programs and encourage them to establish a named fund designed to underwrite and enhance your volunteer recognition efforts. Below is a sample worksheet for identifying costs:

> **What would it take to endow your volunteer recognition program?**
>
> | Existing Costs | Minimum Endowment Gift (Based on 5 Percent Return) |
> |---|---|
> | Annual volunteer recognition program | |
> | Meal $20/person, 200 attendees .$4,000 | |
> | Awards costs (plaques, etc.) ....$1,200 | |
> | Decorations ....$500 | |
> | Invitations ....$500 | |
> | Speaker honorarium......................$1,000 | |
> | Total.........................$7,200 | $145,000* |
>
> **An even more significant endowment gift would allow you to expand your volunteer recognition efforts.*

Calculate what it would take to endow your volunteer recognition efforts.

IDENTIFY ENDOWMENT FUNDING OPPORTUNITIES

Build an Awards Endowment Fund

The list of endowment fund types that can be created is endless. To help your long-term advancement efforts, why not market the idea of establishing an awards endowment?

How would the fund's income be used?

To help cover the costs associated with your annual awards program, seek a donor who would be enthusiastic about establishing an awards endowment.

Annual income would underwrite major costs associated with your awards program: plaques, receptions/banquets honoring awards recipients, printed programs, invitations, publicity, travel/lodging for awards recipients and more.

How would the endowment really help our organization?

The fund would not only provide budget relief to cover current awards costs, but — depending on the size of the fund — would also allow you to enhance your awards program, even creating new awards in line with your mission. You may be able to create regional or statewide awards to honor more noteworthy accomplishments and draw more widespread attention to your organization and its work. In addition to the positive and increased visibility generated, those being honored — perhaps even those associated with honorees — may, with proper cultivation, become major donors.

Who might be interested in establishing an awards endowment?

Turn first to persons already highly committed to your charity and able to appreciate long-term publicity and gift implications you could realize from such a fund. As a more personal benefit, the donor would receive ongoing publicity associated with all future awards — in news releases, printed awards programs, etc. For example: "This award is underwritten through the generosity of the [name of endowed fund]."

Where should we begin?

First, draft a proposal describing existing awards and listing all costs associated with each. Add to it a what-if section enhancing existing awards and illustrating new awards that could be created, along with anticipated costs. The proposal should illustrate awards and associated costs as they now stand, and what you could accomplish in the way of enhanced and new awards with a larger endowment fund.

Endowed Scholarships Aren't Limited to Schools

You need not represent a college, university or school to market endowed scholarships. Many types of nonprofits could make use of this popular endowment opportunity. As long as the named endowment offers some sort of learning experience for the recipient(s), it could be referred to as a scholarship.

Depending on the type of nonprofit you represent, endowed scholarships could be used to:

- Provide summer camp opportunities for youth.
- Offer participation in conferences or workshops for financially deserving individuals.
- Furnish professional development opportunities for employees.
- Cover costs associated with learning travel experiences.
- Teach and train volunteers.
- Underwrite internship experiences.

Create a List Of Outdoor Endowment Possibilities

Do you have naming gift opportunities that may exist outside of your facilities? Many donors are drawn to such funding possibilities. Annual interest from such funds could be used to maintain and enhance designated projects.

Develop a list of naming endowment opportunities for outside projects. Your list may include:

- Landscaping
- Gardens
- Patios
- Fountains
- Walkways
- Lighting
- Recreational sites
- Ponds
- Driveways, parking lots
- Statues or other landmarks
- Trails

IDENTIFY ENDOWMENT FUNDING OPPORTUNITIES

Library Endowment Opportunities

Looking for ways to endow your library? Identify these and other endowment opportunities for those interested in library needs:

Acquisitions endowment — Annual interest used to purchase new books and periodicals. Acquisitions could even be restricted to particular subjects such as natural sciences, research or religion.

Rare books endowment — Underwrites the acquisition and maintenance of your rare books section.

Archives endowment — Many libraries are host to a nonprofit's historical documents and artifacts. Interest from this fund could be used to protect and enhance your archives.

Exhibits endowment — Used to host traveling and permanent library exhibits.

Professional development endowment — The fund would underwrite costs associated with library personnel education and professional development opportunities.

Facilities endowment — Annual proceeds would underwrite the library's physical maintenance and perhaps enhancements as well.

Program endowments — Donors could establish funds to underwrite children's reading programs, literacy programs and more.

Equipment and supplies enhancement fund — Visual aids, software and other needs could be addressed with annual proceeds from this fund.

Lectureship fund — Depending on the amount, proceeds could fund appearances from celebrity speakers, authors and more.

There are any number of restricted endowments that can be established for libraries.

Why Not Market a Goodwill Endowment?

Looking for a named endowment opportunity that donors will love turning into a reality? Consider the merits of encouraging a goodwill or acts of kindness endowment.

How would the annual interest be used? The fund would allow your nonprofit to carry out whatever goodwill acts or community service you and the donor deem appropriate — acts that are in line with your organization's mission and cast it in a favorable light.

An acts of kindness endowment produces a triple win: 1) it enables your organization to conduct community service actions that budget might not otherwise allow; 2) those goodwill acts enhance your organization's image in the community and surrounding area; and 3) the donor gets to make a naming gift that is altruistic in the fullest sense.

Have You Considered an Endowment Loan Fund?

Some nonprofit organizations market loan funds as an endowment gift opportunity. Annual interest from the fund can provide low-interest loans for various purposes: financial assistance to low-income patients, loans to financially deserving students, land acquisition funds for environmental organizations and more.

How is a loan fund different than a traditional endowment fund? Rather than giving away annual interest from the endowment, funds are loaned for a specific purpose with the expectation of the fund being paid back. That's why it is often referred to as a revolving loan fund.

Donors may find a loan fund attractive because of its two-fold value: 1) it provides assistance for deserving recipients or causes and 2) because it's a loan, it teaches fiscal responsibility.

> **Examples of Endowment Loan Funds:**
>
> **The University of Kansas —** www.kuendowment.org/ students/loans/
>
> **Jewish Family and Children's Services** of San Francisco, the Peninsula, Marin and Sonoma Counties: Esther Shiller Memorial Endowment Loan Fund for College Loans — www.jfcs.org

IDENTIFY ENDOWMENT FUNDING OPPORTUNITIES

Any Paid Position Is Endowable

Nearly any employee positions can serve as a unique endowment opportunity for potential donors.

You're familiar with endowed professorships and lectureships, but nearly any paid position could be endowed. The key is the position's attractiveness to potential donors. If you can find someone willing to endow a maintenance position, go for it!

Here are some examples of positions that either have been or could be endowed at various types of not-for-profit organizations:

❑ Nurse ❑ Teacher ❑ Executive Director/CEO
❑ Symphony conductor ❑ Visiting lecturer ❑ Artist in residence
❑ Volunteer manager ❑ Deans of faculty, students, colleges, etc.

How much of an endowment fund is required to underwrite a particular paid position? To arrive at an answer, divide the total annual cost of the position (salary plus benefits) by anticipated annual rate of return required. For example, a $70,000 position would require an endowment of $1.4 million, based on an annual return of 5 percent.

What to Know About Establishing an Endowed Lectureship Program

When marketing endowed lectureships, try to keep its purpose as broad as possible to allow sufficient flexibility in years ahead.

Before establishing an endowed lectureship program, there should be a clear understanding within your organization about needs, rules of engagement when soliciting, and use of funds derived from such a program, says Don Sullivan, provost emeritus, Cameron University (Lawton, OK).

"The endowed lectureships should be compatible with current interests and anticipated thrusts of the organization and not tangents that are of interest to the donor but not compatible with institutional needs," he says. "An endowment should enable both faculty and students to explore new areas and opportunities."

Sullivan addresses questions your organization should know before establishing an endowed lectureship program:

What type of structure and staff should be required before accepting endowed lectureships?

"The endowed lectureship program should already be a routine part of the menu of donor opportunities available through the development office. With a standard endowment agreement in place, the only additional burden for the development office is to finalize an agreement both parties can live with. A development staff member that is knowledgeable of and sensitive to the university's academic programs will be very helpful in this regard.

"Once the endowed lectureship is ready for execution, there must be a defined process for how funds will be administered and the kinds of feedback that will be provided to donors. Cameron University has a process that has proven highly successful. All faculty are apprised about the new lectureship. They must complete a proposal format to compete for the funds. Administration then reviews the proposals to ensure compatibility with both donor intent and academic goals. A final report provides feedback to donors."

Do you have any advice for organizations regarding the acceptance and management of an endowed lectureship?

"Keep the purposes as broad as possible. Since these lectureships are literally forever, it is essential that flexibility be built in regarding how they will be used over the years (including conditions that we cannot even imagine)."

How can an organization determine a minimum amount for establishing an endowed scholarship?

"This depends on the size and type of institution and the environment in which they operate. In Oklahoma's higher education system, endowed lectureships at regional universities like Cameron University are defined as $25,000-$124,999; endowed professorships as $125,000-$249,999; and endowed chairs as $250,000 and above. If the institution meets the minimum threshold through a donor's gift, the Oklahoma State Regents for Higher Education will match the donor gift dollar for dollar. This visionary commitment by the state of Oklahoma (together with foundation matching funds) has been the secret to Cameron University's success."

Source: B. Don Sullivan, Ph.D., Provost Emeritus, Cameron University, Lawton, OK. Phone (580) 581-2999. E-mail: dons@cameron.edu

IDENTIFY ENDOWMENT FUNDING OPPORTUNITIES

Launch an Endow-a-Room Effort

If the organization you represent is characterized by many of the same types of rooms — such as hospital patient rooms, residence hall rooms or musical practice rooms — consider launching an effort to name each room with an appropriate gift.

The annual interest from the gift would be used to underwrite costs associated with that room. At 5 percent, for example, a $25,000 named endowment would provide $1,250 in revenue that could be used for maintenance or room enhancement.

What's good about this type of project fundraising effort? The answer is twofold:

1. Because the size of gift required to endow a room is not overwhelming, the effort will probably generate many first-time major donors who will then become likely candidates for even more significant gifts down the road.

2. It presents many named gift opportunities for building your endowment. A 50-room facility, for instance, could generate $1,250,000 in additional endowment based on $25,000 gifts.

Possible Endow-a-Room Benefits

✓ The donor's name will be placed on the entrance to the room — The John and Betty Doe Room.

✓ A brief bio of the donor(s) will be placed in the room for the benefit of patients or students who use the room.

✓ All donors will be invited to a recognition event in which they will have an opportunity to tour the facility that includes named rooms.

✓ Any future renovations or furnishing enhancements to a room will be followed by an invitation for the donor to visit and see the improvements that have been made.

Offer Endowment Opportunities Tied to Geographic Areas

Do the services of your nonprofit reach beyond your immediate area? Do you have satellite offices, statewide chapters or other types of outreach programs?

If so, consider offering endowment opportunities that will benefit residents of those areas. For example, one statewide agency with chapters in each county encourages residents to establish named endowment funds restricted to their home county.

While you may be inclined to prefer endowment gifts that directly benefit your headquarters, many potential donors might simply choose not to give, believing perhaps that the funds would not benefit projects or people in their immediate area.

Examine the many programs and services you offer outside your immediate area, and come up with a list of endowment opportunities to benefit those who live there. The realization of such endowment funds will allow you to have a greater presence in those outlying locales.

Don't restrict endowment possibilities to your immediate headquarters. Consider the ways in which you serve clients or customers in other communities or regions.

Gifts That Beget Gifts

The Challenge: Finding new ways to create relationships with financially capable (and accomplished) individuals and businesses who presently have no connection to your organization.

One Solution: Create a yearly awards program — one that will capture regional, statewide or even national attention — that fits your organization's mission and honors individuals and/or businesses for particular achievements.

How to Do That: Market a $500,000-or-more named endowment opportunity in which annual interest from the fund would underwrite all expenses associated with a powerful awards program — the awards (e.g., plaques, monetary accolades); the ceremony or event (e.g., invitations to the who's who of your region or state, social hour, dinner); transportation and lodging for awards recipients and their guests, etc.

The Result: Those who visit your yearly event as honorees will have an established connection to your organization by virtue of the award they received. You may even choose to create some sort of society of past award recipients that keeps them officially in the fold.

Identify and Endow Exhibit Opportunities

Does your organization have special exhibits for members or the public?

Consider endowing these exhibit programs to 1) be sure sufficient funding is always available in the future and 2) allow you to enhance exhibit opportunities that may not have been possible in the past.

Exhibit programs provide attractive endowment opportunities because they offer a higher level of visibility for the donor than some other types of endowment gifts. And while a sponsorship may underwrite the cost of a onetime exhibit, annual interest from an exhibit endowment goes on indefinitely.

These and other types of exhibits make great endowment opportunities:

Traveling exhibits — Endowment earnings can cover the cost of transportation and setup from location to location. This allows your organization to provide outreach — and gain greater visibility — to locations beyond your immediate area.

Photographic exhibits — A photographic exhibit could be useful to many types of nonprofit organizations to help educate and increase public awareness of particular issues.

Permanent exhibits — A sufficient endowment may allow your organization to acquire and display more prominent works and items that were previously unaffordable, thus adding to your organization's prominence.

Exhibits need not be limited to museums and art centers. Consider how your organization might justify an ongoing exhibit program to educate, enlighten, attract visitors, expand services and more. Then develop a plan for marketing naming opportunities to endow those programs.

The benefits of endowing exhibits will benefit your organization and those you serve for years to come.

Gifts That Beget Gifts

Gift Opportunity — Establish an outsourcing endowment fund — an endowed gift from which annual interest would be available to cover development-related costs that could be farmed out: consulting fees, electronic screening costs, production of a case statement or campaign literature, etc.

Solution — Create a proposal that 1) identifies outsourcing costs which have been incurred during the past five years to determine the endowment gift size necessary to cover future outsourcing costs and 2) includes additional outsourcing opportunities that have not been carried out — due to budget constraints — but would have a positive impact on your development efforts if funds were available.

Donor Benefits — The donor would take pride in knowing that his/her gift will allow you to move ahead with major gift plans that might not otherwise have been possible: a feasibility study, architectural plans, development of a master plan for your facilities, etc. Such activities would enable your organization to proceed in planning for future growth.

Such a gift could also be considered a lead gift in the planning stages of a capital campaign.

Review your organization's current sponsorship opportunities as potential endowment opportunities.

Endowment Possibilities

What yearly programs or events do you have that are currently underwritten through sponsorships? Make note of them. Then consider each of them as an endowment opportunity. After all, if all existing sponsorships were endowed — covering all future costs associated with those programs or events — that would free up new sponsorship opportunities.

Endowment Builder: Practical Ideas for Securing Endowment Gifts, Second Edition.
Edited by Scott C. Stevenson.
© 2009 Stevenson, Inc. Published 2009 by Stevenson, Inc.

PROSPECT IDENTIFICATION IDEAS AND STRATEGIES

Although endowment gifts may not appeal to everyone, those who do believe in the value of endowment tend to be easily enthused about doing what they can to make such gifts a reality. In addition to identifying new prospects, look to those who have already established named endowments for additional gifts.

Where to Look for Endowment Donors

Not every donor is inclined to contribute to an organization's endowment. That's due partially to the fact that many people don't fully understand how an endowment fund works or the impact it can have on a charity. That's why it helps to know how to identify those persons who are more likely to give to endowment funds.

One approach to discover those individuals: Review the names of persons who have made endowment gifts to other charities in your surrounding area — hospitals, universities, churches and synagogues, art centers, symphonies and more. Ask friends of your organization to share copies of annual reports and contributor lists that they receive as contributors to these charities. Then tag any listed endowment donor who has also made any type of contribution to your cause. These will be among your prime candidates for endowment gifts.

Additionally, identify those persons who have made endowment gifts to other organizations but have made no gift to yours. These, too, will be candidates worthy of cultivation.

Connect With Your Community's Native Sons and Daughters

Based on the type of nonprofit you represent — your mission, programs and services — could you justify a program intended to connect with former residents of your community — people who were born or grew up there but now live elsewhere?

Find a sincere way to connect with native sons and daughters and there's no limit on what you can do to cultivate relationships with financially capable individuals who are part of this group.

Here are some examples of how you might cultivate relationships with your city's or state's natives:

1. **Start a who's who of your city or service region.** Work at building a list of natives who have gone on to achieve success and any degree of celebrity. This becomes your working list of those to be approached and cultivated. Talk to old-timers who can help identify those persons. Visit with the alumni offices of your city's colleges, universities and schools to identify their who's who lists. Talk to chamber of commerce officials to see if such a list already exists in their office. You may even decide to form a who's who advisory committee to help with this undertaking.

2. **Identify ways to reconnect natives with their hometown (or state).** Share news clippings, historical accounts and more. Involve old friends and relatives to help re-establish ties and make introductions with your organization.

3. **Take the lead in establishing a yearly event that invites former residents back.** If a community festival of some sort already exists, use that as a homecoming connecting point.

4. **Initiate an annual awards program that selects community natives based on their achievements.** You may choose to collaborate with your local chamber or other organizations to make this program more encompassing.

5. **Build a Web page geared to your community's native sons and daughters.** Share your who's who list on the site and include brief biographies on each or limit them to past awards recipients. Include links to your community's history and points of interest. Offer trivia questions about your community to which visitors can respond. Include a gallery of former residents' photos.

Pursue Family Gifts

Rather than going after a single major gift, consider approaching members of an extended family for a naming gift that honors a patriarch and/or matriarch. Here's why:

1. **Multiple gifts help to maximize both number and size of gifts.** There can be a motivating synergy — and sometimes even competition — that takes place when family members pull together to establish a combined fund.

2. **Family gifts create generations of giving.** If you have one donor and that donor dies, you have lost a donor. If you cultivate a family through succeeding generations, giving will likely continue after the lead donor's death.

3. **Family gifts create opportunity for ongoing cultivation.** This is especially so for donor-advised funds that require regular contact between the charity and family members involved.

4. **Your sphere of public awareness expands as your donor list grows.** Instead of having one donor telling others of his/her association with your organization, you have multiple family members extolling your organization's virtues.

5. **Jointly established family gifts help encourage other families to do the same.** If you publicize and market realized family gifts, others will take note and consider doing the same.

PROSPECT IDENTIFICATION IDEAS AND STRATEGIES

Nurture Board Gifts by Inspiring Your Board Members

Your foundation board or board of trustees needs to back a major gifts program completely and enthusiastically. After all, these are the persons who should be raising the bar for others who will one day invest significantly in your cause.

That's why it's important that board members become and remain inspired about what major gifts can and will do for your organization.

To energize board members, use these and other approaches:

1. Invite someone who has made a major gift to your nonprofit or another charity to speak to your board about the personal rewards of such gifts.

2. Conduct an exercise in which board members discuss how they would use a windfall $5 million gift for your charity. After hearing and recording their dreams, invite the board to spend some time discussing what it would take to secure $5 million in gifts.

3. Invite the CEO and/or board chair of another nonprofit — one with an exemplary history of major gifts — to meet with your board and talk about how large gifts have impacted his/her organization and those it serves.

4. Develop a list of institutions to which you aspire — those with significant endowments, new and enhanced facilities, state-of-the-art equipment and cutting edge programs. Share the comparative list at each board meeting to demonstrate what could be realized with more major gifts.

Bringing your board members to a new level of gift expectations is a long-term process. Persist in your quest to make believers of them.

Your board members' involvement in and enthusiasm for your endowment efforts will set the tone for inspiring others to invest.

Content not available in this edition

Simple Form Helps Identify Major Donors, Prompts Follow-up Development Efforts

Are you ready to move from raising mid-level gifts to bringing in major gifts to support your nonprofit? Here's how a simple form is helping a nonprofit accomplish just that:

Mary Louise Everhart, director of development, Conestoga Christian School (Morgantown, PA) says she is "taking baby steps toward a major giving program by using simple inquiry forms (shown at left) to ask board members to help identify potential donors of means.

"People can be hesitant to invest their personal relationships in fundraising," Everhart says. "This gives them another avenue to make suggestions, even if not from within their own sphere of influence."

Everhart and her staff send the forms periodically with board packets. The forms ask board members to share information about prospective donors, including why they might be a good match for the school, what area of giving might suit them best and giving potential.

The form helps board members keep fundraising on their radar, "and it lets them know that we are doing the same in the development office," she says.

As the program grows, Everhart says she hopes to implement a system of calling on three prospective donors per month.

Source: Mary Louise Everhart, Director of Development, Conestoga Christian School, Morgantown, PA. Phone (610) 286-0353. E-mail: marylouise.everhart@conestogachristian.net

PROSPECT IDENTIFICATION IDEAS AND STRATEGIES

Nurture Endowment Giving Among Up-and-comers

You no doubt have a constituency of younger individuals who will one day be in a position to make significant gifts but can't do so quite yet. To educate those up-and-comers and prepare them for that day when they can make a major gift, take the following steps:

1. Form a committee made up of dedicated younger donors and ask them to develop a list of persons they would be willing to contact for affordable gifts. (If each donor could make a pledge of $1,000 over a two- or three-year period, and you could get 30 participants, you would end up with a $30,000 endowment fund.)

2. Launch a group endowment project that has appeal to your younger donors and invite these donors to collectively support the project. Let committee members have a say in selecting the project.

3. Once the endowment has been fully funded, involve those participants in witnessing the impact of the fund on your organization and those you serve. Communicate with them regularly on the fund's status and what it is accomplishing each year.

Over time, these donors will come to appreciate how an endowment works and become likely candidates to establish their own named endowments when they are more financially capable.

Recognize that younger constituents are also capable of making endowment gifts.

Use Cold Calls to Identify Mutual Interests

When making introductory calls on prospects, use the opportunity to identify those characteristics your prospect has in common with your organization and its mission. Those common characteristics — beliefs, perceptions, interests, values — will be used to build a long-term relationship over time. What your organization has in common with a prospect will impact his/her proclivity to invest in your cause.

To effectively identify traits your organization may have in common with a prospect, it's important to easily identify those traits. To help accomplish that, create a checklist of your organization's most distinguishing characteristics. Then, after each meeting with a new prospect, pinpoint what he/she has in common with your charity.

To the right is a sample worksheet for comparing an organization's characteristics with those of a prospective donor to find common ground on which to build a relationship.

WINDEMERE ACADEMY

Development Officer: Mark Russell Date: 11/12/08

Prospect's Name: John Langdon, Owner: Langdon Plumbing

Windemere Academy Characteristics	Prospect's Similar Characteristics	Comments
Belief in private education		
Disciplines _____ Art _____ Business Tech _____ Computer Science _____ English/Social Studies _____ Foreign Language _____ Health _____ Language Arts _____ Mathematics _____ Science _____ Social Studies		
Belief in philanthropy		
Community betterment		
Christian values		
Commitment to service		
Strong work ethic		
Politically conservative		

Endowment Builder: Practical Ideas for Securing Endowment Gifts, Second Edition.
Edited by Scott C. Stevenson.
© 2009 Stevenson, Inc. Published 2009 by Stevenson, Inc.

STRATEGIES FOR MARKETING ENDOWMENT GIFTS

Those organizations having experienced the greatest success in building their endowments have done so by promoting such gifts in a variety of capacities. The following sampling of ideas will help you identify new and improved ways of marketing endowment gifts.

Develop a Wish List of Endowment Opportunities

Are you sharing a wide array of endowment opportunities with potential donors or limiting yourself to a handful of possibilities? Here are some examples of endowment ideas to add to your wish list:

A variety of endowment possibilities will allow donors and prospects to select the option that best suits their interests.

✓ **Outreach endowment** — Gifts allow you to bring your programs and services beyond your community.

✓ **Public awareness endowment** — Gifts could fund an awareness campaign, advertising and other efforts not covered by the general budget.

✓ **Acquisitions fund** — Would purchase books, supplies, artwork or other needs not covered by your general budget.

✓ **Lecture/speakers series** — Interest would pay to bring distinguished speakers to address topics of interest.

✓ **Retired employees fund** — Interest could provide some type of benefits to longtime employees who have retired after years of service, enhancing their standing as emeritus faculty or former employees.

✓ **Professional development fund** — This fund could pay for continuing education and professional learning for staff or departments.

✓ **Scholarship endowment** — In addition to traditional scholarships, donors could establish named endowments directed to those you serve: travel experiences, internships, youth camps, etc.

✓ **Venture capital fund** — Annual interest would encourage entrepreneurial efforts that address your mission.

✓ **Technology enhancement fund** — Permits upgrading/installation of computers, software, equipment and more.

✓ **Stewardship fund** — Income funds items not in general budget: flowers for holidays or funerals, donor appreciation events, donor plaques, etc.

✓ **Landscape/beautification endowment** — Provides for outdoor enhancement: trees, shrubs, parking, walkways, fountains, signage, more.

✓ **Building maintenance fund** — Covers ongoing maintenance of specific buildings or rooms.

✓ **Awards endowment** — Underwrites costs associated with awards provided by your nonprofit: achievement, community service, volunteer and more.

Look for New Ways to Promote Endowment Gifts

To encourage more endowment gifts, keep exploring new and expanded ways to aggressively promote them. Here's a sampling of strategies worth using:

To realize more endowment gifts keep exploring new funding opportunities and ways of telling your story.

1. Set a specific endowment increase over a three- to-five-year period, then promote it.

2. Convince a foundation or individual to establish an endowment challenge to match all endowment gifts made over a specified time period.

3. Expand naming endowment gift opportunities: landscaping, programs, positions, etc.

4. Have a board-approved policy in place automatically designating all unrestricted bequests to your endowment.

5. Never end a meeting without mentioning something related to endowment goals.

6. In addition to a planned gifts club, create one for anyone who establishes a named endowment.

7. Always make mention of endowment issues at board meetings.

STRATEGIES FOR MARKETING ENDOWMENT GIFTS

Don't Miss Opportunity to Market Endowment Gifts

It happens all the time: Someone who has served as CEO of a nonprofit for 25 years announces plans to retire; to recognize the person's longtime service, the board of trustees decides to name a building in his/her honor.

While this is a meaningful gesture, all too often organizers fail to see the opportunity as more and neglect to invite the public to endow the newly named facility.

If your organization decides to name a facility (or even a portion of a building) in someone's honor based on that individual's significant contributions of service, use that limited time window to seek endowment gifts, the annual interest from which can be used to maintain and even enhance the facility.

Here's some of what you can do when naming a facility in honor of someone:

1. Host a major reception in the facility honoring that person.

2. Work with the honoree to come up with an extensive list of invitees and give those names a special code in your database — for follow-up purposes.

3. Use the reception (or receptions) as an opportunity to recognize the honoree, to publicly announce the naming of that facility and to publicly invite attendees to consider making a three-year pledge to endow the maintenance of that facility.

4. Use reception time to offer facility tours.

5. Following the reception(s), work with your board to review the list invitees and ask for board members' assistance in making calls on the most financially capable guests for the purpose of soliciting endowment pledges.

Keep in mind: If you are naming an entire facility in honor of someone, you might offer naming opportunities within the facility (e.g., offices, lobby areas, patient or classrooms) to those who make endowment gifts at a certain level.

Don't miss milestone opportunities such as anniversaries, retirements and building dedications to market your endowment gift options.

Ratchet Up Endowments With 5-Year Marketing Plan

Charities often launch capital campaigns that include an endowment component, but how about a full-fledged effort focused on endowment only? Create a plan to ratchet up endowment gifts.

An endowment plan is similar to a yearly fundraising operational plan that includes one or more goals, quantifiable objectives that address those goals, accompanying action plans that spell out fundraising strategies and a timetable that lists what should occur when and who's responsible.

Start with a realistic yet challenging goal based on a review of prospects and past fundraising history. Seek input from those whose financial participation will help you achieve your goal. And by all means, be sure your board takes full ownership of the entire process.

This is a simplified five-year endowment plan. An actual plan requires far more detail; also, timetable is not shown.

5-Year Endowment Plan • Goal: Raise $8 million in endowment gifts by 2014.

Objective No. 1: Secure $5 million through planned gifts and planned gift expectancies by 2014.

Objective No. 2: Secure $3 million in outright gifts by 2014.

Action Plan 1-A: *Prospect calls program* Identify, research, cultivate and track no fewer than 200 qualified planned gift prospects over a five-year period.

Action Plan 1-B: *Heritage Society* Establish and manage a planned gifts society to recognize and steward those who have established planned gifts.

Action Plan 1-C: *Quarterly newsletter* Produce and distribute quarterly planned gifts newsletter to all planned gift prospects.

Action Plan 1-D: *Estate planning seminars* Coordinate no fewer than two estate planning seminars per fiscal year in an effort to identify and cultivate planned gifts.

Action Plan 1-E: *Planned gifts committee* Assemble and manage planned gifts committee that approves planned gift policies and assisting in identifying, cultivating and soliciting planned gifts.

Action Plan 2-A: *Endowment Committee* Recruit and manage an endowment committee responsible for assisting in the identification, cultivation and solicitation of outright endowment gifts.

Action Plan 2-B: *Prospect calls program* Manage the identification, research, cultivation and solicitation of no fewer than 200 qualified major gift prospects over a five-year period.

Action Plan 2-C: *Communications program* Develop an endowment marketing piece (and peripheral publications) designed to help in marketing planned gifts.

Action Plan 2D: *Naming gift opportunities* Develop endowment naming gift opportunities from which prospects can choose.

STRATEGIES FOR MARKETING ENDOWMENT GIFTS

Explore Endowment Possibilities With Your Constituents

Craft an introductory endowment brochure to inform prospects about your endowment fund and the benefits associated with the program.

What are you currently doing to make constituents aware of how they can make endowment gifts to your cause? Are they familiar with the possibilities that exist?

You may find a simple introductory brochure helpful for illustrating the many choices available when establishing named endowed funds. Although you may offer more detailed or customized literature later in the cultivation process, a simple piece that illustrates funding possibilities can be helpful in getting prospects to visualize themselves as major donors. It will help prospects see how annual interest from their endowed funds would make a noticeable difference for your cause and those it serves.

An introductory brochure such as the sample below also points out the minimum donation required to establish an endowed fund for your cause. Plus, it illustrates various ways in which one can fulfill a pledge, illustrating that major gifts can be affordable for many who wish to invest in your organization's long-range plans.

In addition, this format shows prospects your organization's total anticipated needs in various categories. Although donors have the option of establishing named funds for lesser amounts within a particular category, there may be those who choose to fund an entire need on their own.

Sample introductory brochure used to introduce endowment gift opportunities.

Help Ensure Our Children's Future — Establish a Named Endowment

You can make a world of difference for generations to come by establishing a named endowment fund through the Jefferson School Foundation. Annual income from your endowment will provide valuable and ongoing tools necessary to prepare Jefferson students for life's goals.

JEFFERSON SCHOOL FOUNDATION JSF

Although named endowment funds begin at $10,000 — since only a portion of the fund's annual interest is used to fund intended programs — donors can establish such funds over a period of time if they so choose. For example, a donor could:

- Pledge to contribute funds over an agreed-to number of years until the fund reaches a particular amount.
- Pledge to contribute funds over a number of years and then add to the fund through a planned gift.
- Make an irrevocable planned gift which will commence after the lifetime of the donor.
- Make a one-time, outright gift of $10,000 or more to fully fund a particular program or project.

Below is a small sampling of some endowment funds you may wish to consider establishing. Please keep in mind, donors may establish named funds for as little as $10,000 for any program/project even though the total needed for that program/project far exceeds that amount.

Travel Fund
Total Endowment Needed: $250,000

Often students qualify to participate in some academic or extracurricular experience that requires travel but they are unable to cover associated costs — lodging, meals, transportation, entry fees, etc. This fund would help ensure that every student can participate regardless of his/her family's financial circumstances.

Technology Fund
Total Endowment Needed: $500,000

Annual interest from the establishment of this fund would allow our school to make needed computer and related equipment purchases and, equally important, provide funding to cover maintenance of such equipment.

Endowed Positions
Total Endowment Needed: $1 million

Funds established in this category would underwrite the total cost of particular positions at Jefferson — both existing or new positions. Annual interest would cover salary and benefits and help ensure that our school attracts top professionals from throughout the region and nation.

Post-secondary Scholarships
Total Endowment Needed: Unlimited

Annual scholarship awards to graduating seniors will help guarantee that our graduates continue the tradition of educational preparedness they received as Jefferson students.

High School Internships
Total Endowment Needed: $50,000

Annual interest from this fund would be used to make internship possibilities more accessible to juniors/seniors during the academic year as well as summer months.

Teachers' Professional Development Fund
Total Endowment Needed: $150,000

Annual interest would be awarded for learning/continuing education to deserving teachers.

Capital Improvements/Maintenance Fund
Total Endowment Needed: $1 million

Annual interest from this category would be used for needed capital improvements to the school as well as covering maintenance of the facilities and grounds.

STRATEGIES FOR MARKETING ENDOWMENT GIFTS

Gift Cards Encourage New Gifts to Endowed Funds

Enclosing gift cards in annual stewardship reports encourages new donations to Wake Forest University Baptist Medical Center (Winston-Salem, NC).

The gift cards (see below) include a paragraph that reads: "If you would like to continue to make the Dr. Charlie Brown Scholarship Fund an even greater resource for our dedicated medical students, please feel free to share the enclosed gift cards with your friends and family," and provide information on how to obtain additional cards.

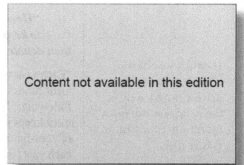

The simple tool is increasing awareness and donor numbers, says Erika A. Friedel, director of donor relations. For instance, one couple who endowed a research fund in memory of their daughter asked for 200 more cards. Another donor who has a research fund in memory of his wife requested 100 cards to share with family and friends.

"We raised $23,380 via gift cards from 70 constituents last fiscal year," Friedel says. Plus, "one donor sent $20,000 via a gift card to augment his endowed fund."

The cards are produced in-house using perforated card stock preprinted with the medical center name and logo. The layout is created using a Microsoft Word template that can be changed to note a specific donor's endowed fund, brief history and the fund's restriction code to make it easier to record the gifts and cards when they arrive.

Source: Erika A. Friedel, Director of Donor Relations, Office of Development & Alumni Affairs, Wake Forest University Baptist Medical Center, Winston-Salem, NC. Phone (800) 899-7128. E-mail: efriedel@wfubmc.edu

Vary Ways You Market Endowment Opportunities

How are endowment opportunities being promoted by your organization?

Too often, charities use only one or two methods to get the word out. To make sure you are reaching your various publics in a variety of ways, market your organization's endowment opportunities through these and other methods:

- Articles in your planned gifts and general newsletters.

- A specific direct mail appeal — with a bounce back — that invites recipients to respond and explore options.

- Features and news releases that discuss various aspects of your endowment.

- Receptions hosted by those who have established endowed funds.

STRATEGIES FOR MARKETING ENDOWMENT GIFTS

Boosting Endowment Gifts

"How do you get donors to increase their investment to their endowment funds to keep pace with the rising cost of tuition and fees (which are currently more than double the inflation rate)?"

Finding new and creative ways to keep donors engaged in their endowment fund investments is vital to future gifts.

"Each year we send a letter and endowment report to donors or representatives of our endowment funds that includes a veiled request for additional funds. This year's letter included the following: 'By continuing to make gifts to your endowment, you can ensure that your endowment keeps pace with the rising cost of providing higher education. Your gifts increase the value of your fund, thereby increasing the amount available to award and the number of awards made each year.' Although we've toyed with the idea of including a return envelope, we have not done so and have learned from other professionals that it is not a good idea. "

— *Rainy Stephenson, Stewardship Manager, Oakland University, John Dodge House (Rochester, MI)*

"If at all possible, it's best to discuss this in person with the donor. In my 11 years as a development officer, I've found it helpful to frame the award in the context of a student's total expense. For example: 'Expenses for a full-time student are $5,000. Your fund currently generates $500 (10 percent of tuition).' If you have the historical information, you can even illustrate that, years ago, the scholarship covered 50 percent (or whatever) of a student's expense."

— *Amy Margaret Sajko, Former Director of Development, College of Business, Illinois State University (Normal, IL)*

Four Ways to Draw More Attention to Endowment Gifts

To make endowment giving a more visible gift option, make use of these methods:

1. **Utilize benchmarking.** Make comparisons of your endowment with similar recognized leaders — those nonprofits to which you aim to aspire. Share those comparisons with your constituency.

2. **Draw attention to existing endowment gifts.** Distribute news and feature stories about donors, present and past, who have made endowment gifts to your charity. How are they impacting those you serve? How were those endowment gifts funded — stocks, bequests, cash?

3. **Share endowment fund possibilities.** Produce a handout of endowment gift opportunities that also lists all existing named endowment funds at your institution or agency. Include that list on your website.

4. **Encourage planned endowment gifts.** Endowment gifts often come about through planned gifts: bequests, charitable annuities, life insurance and more. Promote endowment gifts through your planned gifts newsletter, during face-to-face visits and in direct mail.

Million-dollar Challenge Helps Build Endowment Fund

To help build a newly established endowment fund, a board member and chairman emeritus for the Character Education Partnership (CEP) of Washington, DC, issued a challenge: "Raise $3 million and I will gift $1 million."

The challenge came after extensive homework by persons doing the asking, says Lee MacVaugh, director of development and fundraising.

"This particular board member has been our chairman for 13 years and is very committed to our nonprofit. Because he has been so generous to our cause in the past, I wanted to make sure we weren't over-asking and burdening him with requests," says MacVaugh. "We came to the conclusion the ask should be for our newly created endowment fund.

"It only took him a few moments to ponder the idea before he issued the challenge," MacVaugh adds.

In a little over two months, the board member's challenge has led to four gifts totaling more than $150,000 and seven pledges from other board members.

"Meeting this challenge is very important for our organization," says MacVaugh. "I read once that donors like to give to organizations that are financially sound. If we can show $4 million in the bank, it will show prospective donors that CEP is financially secure and will be around for years to come."

He says the CEP has begun promoting the challenge through its website, mailings, donor meetings and annual report and will do so in future publications.

Source: Lee MacVaugh, Director of Development and Fundraising, Character Education Partnership, Washington, DC. Phone (202) 296-7743, ext. 14. E-mail: lmacvaugh@character.org

STRATEGIES FOR MARKETING ENDOWMENT GIFTS

Develop a Well-thought-out Endowment Handout

To show would-be donors that you are serious about the importance of gifts to your endowment, take the time to develop an attractive and comprehensive brochure that covers key components of endowment giving.

Your brochure or booklet may include but not be limited to:

✓ **List of existing named funds** — This list, which may include photos of the donors, serves as a great marketing tool in two respects: It motivates would-be donors to establish funds of their own and it recognizes existing donors and encourages them to add to their funds.

✓ **Examples of endowment's impact** — How is your current endowment positively impacting your organization and those you serve? How are individual named endowments making a difference?

✓ **A list of named fund opportunities** — A wish list of available opportunities that, along with the minimum cost of establishing each fund, gives donors choices and can help pinpoint funding interests.

✓ **Endowment history and performance** — Use the handout as an opportunity to educate the public about your endowment. Informed individuals are more likely to make a significant investment.

✓ **Benchmarking goals** — Don't hesitate to compare your endowment to similar organizations to which you aspire. Use charts to illustrate differences between your charity's and others' endowments.

✓ **Biographical information about your investment committee and endowment manager** — Show would-be donors that their gifts will be well-stewarded by respected and competent individuals.

✓ **Strategic plan summary** — Summarize those portions of your strategic plan that help substantiate the importance of a growing endowment.

✓ **Description of types of gifts used to establish named endowments** — Describe the various ways in which endowment gifts can be funded (e.g., cash, securities, property). Also distinguish between outright and various types of planned gifts (e.g., bequests, charitable gift annuities).

✓ **Testimonials** — Incorporate some testimonials from those who have established endowment funds. These brief quotes may be included in your list of existing funds.

✓ **Organizational achievements** — People want to know they are investing with a winner. Share specific achievements your charity has made in recent years. List ways that demonstrate you are a good steward of their gifts (e.g., number of consecutive years of balanced budgets).

✓ **Action steps** — Point out the steps anyone can take to explore endowment gifts. Whom do they contact? Stress the confidentiality of all inquiries.

To help would-be donors take a more in-depth look at endowment gifts, take time to develop a comprehensive brochure highlighting various aspects of your endowment, gift opportunities and the impact of endowment gifts.

Investment Committee's Role in Promoting Endowment Gifts

Boards of many nonprofit organizations include an investment or finance committee that is charged with overseeing decisions and policies governing endowment investments. And for many of those committees, that's where the responsibilities end. In their minds, anything that has to do with promoting or soliciting gifts is the sole responsibility of the development committee. But it shouldn't be that way.

Help your board's finance or investment committee realize the full extent of their responsibilities. List those obligations in the committee description, including service as endowment ambassadors to:

• Educate the public on the importance of endowment and what they can do to help it grow.

• Serve as centers of influence in identifying prospects and sharing those names with appropriate development staff.

• Assist in making introductions and cultivating friends and associates.

• Assist in the solicitation of endowment gifts.

• Assist in stewarding existing donors who have invested in the endowment.

Because all of your board members should assume responsibilities in fund development, these additional duties will make your finance or investment committee's responsibilities more official.

STRATEGIES FOR MARKETING ENDOWMENT GIFTS

Showcase Major Gift Needs Between Campaigns

Use the time between your organization's capital campaigns to focus on endowment needs.

Who says major gift fundraising should halt between capital campaigns? Although most consultants advocate gearing up for the next campaign the minute one ends, there are nonprofits that so successfully raise major gifts continually that they can go for years without launching a formal capital campaign.

Showcasing major gift opportunities is not unlike creating a wish list often used in conjunction with an annual fund effort. It's just on a bigger scale.

Seek input from your organization's employees in creating a prioritized gift opportunities list. Consult with board members and past donors to gain insight into their perceptions of institutional needs. Rely on your existing strategic plan to help prioritize funding opportunities. Then, develop a major gifts wish list made up of endowment, bricks and mortar, programming and equipment opportunities. Many of the gift needs may represent naming opportunities; others may not.

Incorporate the list into a marketing piece such as the one shown here for you to use when making individual calls.

Below is a sample wish list page that might be incorporated into a gift opportunities publication.

CONSEQUENTIAL GIFT OPPORTUNITIES 2007-09

EXISTING ENDOWMENT OPPORTUNITIES

Named endowment opportunities require a gift (or gift commitment) of $25,000 or more. Gifts of lesser amounts may be directed to existing endowment funds. Current named endowment opportunities include:

- Scholarships .... $25,000 or more

Facility Maintenance and Enhancement Funds
- Auditorium $100,000
- Wellness and Exercise Center $250,000
- Individual Offices .... $ 25,000

Outdoor Endowment Opportunities
- Garden Area West of Administration Building .... $ 30,000
- Primary Entrance Road $250,000

NEW EQUIPMENT OPPORTUNITIES
- Computer Lab Replacement Fund .... $ 60,000
- Science Lab Enhancement $110,000
- Organ Replacement $250,000

NEW PROGRAM OPPORTUNITIES
- Creation of a Travel Abroad Program $125,000
- Enhance Career Development Internship Program ... $ 50,000

NEW RENOVATION OPPORTUNITIES
- Chapel Tower Replacement $500,000
- Addition of Elevator to Library $150,000
- Handicapped Accessible Improvements $300,000
- Refurbishing Classrooms (Individual) .... $ 20,000

Endowment Marketing Idea

Companies do it: "Lifetime guarantee." Why can't you? When marketing endowment gifts, include the catch-phrase: "*Lifetime* Guarantee!"

Ask Everyone for Endowment Support

Don't write off anyone when it comes to endowment support. Invite everyone on your mailing list to support endowment efforts.

Do you ever make a point to ask everyone on your mailing list for an endowment gift? Even if it's a separate direct mail appeal, everyone should be asked to give to your endowment from time to time. Why? Two reasons:

1. An endowment appeal helps to build your endowment over time.

2. Regardless of gift size, your endowment appeal helps to identify those with an interest in endowment. Once you know who they are, you can work at cultivating larger named gifts over time.

Endowment Builder: Practical Ideas for Securing Endowment Gifts, Second Edition.
Edited by Scott C. Stevenson.
© 2009 Stevenson, Inc. Published 2009 by Stevenson, Inc.

CULTIVATION: BUILDING THE CASE FOR SUPPORT

The realization of significant endowment gifts can take time. They will come in the form of both outright and planned gifts. They are the culmination of a relationship-building process that demands the highest level of honesty and integrity.

Emphasize Endowment Gifts' Immortality Factor

Some donors, particularly those who are attracted to endowment giving, take comfort in recognizing the immortality of their generosity. Part of their rationale for supporting endowment is the fact that their gift will continue doing its work long after their lives end. That's reason enough to think about and practice incorporating the immortality factor into any endowment solicitation.

Use these more universal phrases as a basis for developing those that are more in line with your organization and its mission:

"Imagine the hundreds of lives your gift will touch as time goes on!"

"Even those who are not yet born will one day know your name and be grateful for your foresight."

"Unlike a named building that may not be around generations from now, your named endowment will continue to benefit others far into the future."

"I can think of no nobler way to be remembered."

Help donors understand the perpetuity of endowment gifts.

Cultivation Menu Helps Explore Next Moves

Going after major gifts often requires a much more sophisticated series of cultivation moves than required for lower-end gifts. And because you can't use the same friend-raising strategies with every prospect — they should be tailored to the interests and circumstances of each — it's important to select from many alternatives.

To help you plan individualized cultivation moves for each of your major gift prospects, develop a menu of cultivation categories, such as the example at right, to guide you in your decision making. These categories can be used as a tool by individual development officers or in a group setting as a way of brainstorming what cultivation moves would be most appropriate with particular prospects.

Use of a cultivation possibilities menu also forces you to ask, "What's my most important objective with this prospect at this point in time?"

CULTIVATION POSSIBILITIES MENU

Prospect Under Consideration _____ Date _____

Objective   **Steps To Be Taken**

To involve one or more family members of the prospect....
1. _____
2. _____

To recognize or honor the prospect....
1. _____
2. _____

To help the prospect more fully understand and appreciate the work of our organization....
1. _____
2. _____

To make the prospect more aware of the level of gift required....
1. _____
2. _____

To better determine the prospect's potential funding interests....
1. _____
2. _____

To engage the prospect in realizing greater ownership of our agency and its programs....
1. _____
2. _____

Other objectives/steps....
1. _____
2. _____

CULTIVATION: BUILDING THE CASE FOR SUPPORT

Want a Mega Gift? Create a Mega Plan

While most nonprofits would be elated to receive a $1 million or multimillion-dollar gift, many are unwilling to invest the time necessary for cultivating such gifts.

But such a plan needn't be overwhelming. If you invest as little as one day a week identifying and cultivating one or more prospects capable of giving seven- or eight-figure gifts, wouldn't it be worth the sacrifice?

A plan to cultivate mega gifts doesn't necessarily need to be complicated. Having the courage to move forward with an ask is probably more crucial.

Here are five strategies to focus on identifying and cultivating "the big one."

1. **Enlist a competent and committed major gifts committee.** Assemble a committee of big-thinking and accomplished individuals who are willing to help develop ways of approaching would-be donors capable of contributing $1 million or more.

2. **Identify top prospects and conduct sufficient research.** Once you have identified mega gift prospects, take steps to learn as much about them as is reasonable. What you learn may provide the clues that connect them to your organization.

3. **Enlist key centers of influence.** Identify individuals who are already committed to your organization and can play key roles at influencing your top prospects.

4. **Identify prospect's agents of wealth** — Those professionals who serve your prospect (e.g., estate planning attorneys, trust officers) to determine roles they might play in supporting your effort to approach and solicit the prospect.

5. Based on what you learned about each prospect, **develop an individualized plan of introduction and cultivation** leading toward the realization of a major gift.

Although the entire process may take as long as 36 months before formal solicitation is scheduled to occur, you will have created a viable plan for securing the mega gifts your charity wants and deserves.

PROSPECT CULTIVATION PLAN

Name __Susan Eldridge__

Residence __13 Riveredge Estates__
City __Atlanta__   State __GA__   Zip __30350__
Phone __(404) 278-5505__

Second Residence __#2 Country Club Blvd.__
City __Carmel__   State __CA__   Zip __93912__
Phone __(408) 567-5050__

Occupation/Title __Retired CEO__

Place of Employment __Harbaugh Enterprises, Inc.__
Business Address __1545 Peachtree__
City __Atlanta__   State __GA__   Zip __30350__
Phone __(404) 278-8555__

Preferred Email(s) __se@harbaugh.com__
Mobile Phone __(404) 851-3351__

Marital Status: ☒ Married   ☐ Single   ☐ Divorced
Spouse/Significant Other __Harker Eldridge__

Identified Centers of Influence

1. Don Livingston	2. Emma Lamer
3. Mary Turner	4. Matthew Martin
5. Eldon Savage	6. Margaret Baldwin

Identified Agents of Wealth

Attorney Sarah Williamson	Broker Parson Hicks
CPA Gene Larkin	Other
Finan. Planner	Other

Key Cultivation Strategies	Anticipated Timing	Key Players
Dinner w/CEO H Smith	Oct/2008	CEO/Livingston
Mtg w/students/CEO	Dec/2008	CEO/Livingston
Award Honorary Doc.	May/2009	Bd/Faculty
Invite to join bd.	Sept/2009	Bd Chair/CEO
Share initial prop.	Feb/2010	CEO/Livingston

Essential Profile Information:
Eldridge is a self-made millionaire who acquired her wealth through publishing and real estate development. She has one child who is in his 50s and has had health problems throughout life. Eldridge is politically progressive and believes strongly in a liberal arts education. Sold the business in '06 to German company for $320 million.

CULTIVATION: BUILDING THE CASE FOR SUPPORT

Don't Forget to Cultivate Board Members' Spouses

It's rare that a board member will make a major gift decision with no input from their spouse. In some instances, in fact, the board member's spouse may be more inclined to make a major gift than the board member. That's why it's important to pay particular attention to board members' spouses.

Actions such as these will help strengthen ties with board members' spouses:

✓ Whenever you have a board member orientation, include spouses in your program. Use a portion of the experience to educate and another to entertain.

✓ Instead of doing the typical board profile article in your newsletter or magazine, do one that focuses on both spouses.

✓ Consult with a handful of board spouses and come up with a volunteer project that all board spouses can get behind and support.

✓ Unless asked to do differently, always include both spouses in any gift-related discussions.

In many instances, the cultivation of a board member's spouse may be equally, if not more important than that which occurs with the board member.

Periodic Letter From the CEO Helps to Set the Stage

Case Study: A rather small agency has a limited history of gift support. The organization has relied heavily on government funding to carry out services in the past, but officials are concerned that funding won't be there in the future. So the board has decided to focus its efforts on building an endowment over the next several years. With a nearly nonexistent endowment at present, how should they go about cultivating major gift prospects' interest in making endowment gifts to the agency?

Sample quarterly cultivation letter from an agency's CEO to endowment prospects.

Partial Solution: Issue a quarterly letter from the CEO to top endowment prospects. Because raising endowment is a long-term effort, part of the job will be to educate and cultivate the public — particularly the most financially capable — on why and how they should invest in the agency's endowment. One component of the solution, therefore, would be to create a very select mailing list of the community's or region's top prospects and send a quarterly personalized letter to each from agency's CEO.

Although personal visits will be an imperative part of the cultivation process, this quarterly letter from the agency's CEO provides one additional way of educating and nurturing endowment interest in an ongoing fashion. It keeps the agency's presence in the minds of these more capable prospects and provides a steady stream of persuasion. It is not intended as a direct solicitation device.

Depending on the number of prospects who receive the quarterly letter, you may wish to add a more personalized paragraph to each letter. If that's not realistic, your CEO may wish to add a personal greeting on certain letters when signing them. Even the simple addition of a personal signature may not be realistic, however, if your numbers are too large.

Dear <Name>:

Once again I'm writing to you because I believe it's important you know about our agency's work and some of the challenges that lie before us.

Did you know that an agency such as ours should have an endowment in place equal to at least 2.5 times its annual operating budget? With an operating budget of more than $850,000, we should have an endowment of at least $2,125,000, based on that guideline. Our endowment currently stands at $24,700.

Because our agency is only 12 years old, and because it has carried out needed services with the assistance of government funds, the issue of "endowment" was never a pressing priority. But now it is.

There is no assurance that government assistance will be available in the future, but we certainly know that our services will be desperately needed. And that's why our board is making it a top priority to build an endowment fund over the next months and years. We owe it to those we serve to assist them regardless of where funding originates.

Here are a few reasons why we must continue to respond to our community's needs:

[• List compelling statistics/facts here]

I will continue to update you on our agency and efforts to generate endowment support. I also hope we might visit at some point to discuss your possible participation in this important effort.

Sincerely,

<CEO's Name>

CULTIVATION: BUILDING THE CASE FOR SUPPORT

Stress Endowment Gifts' Importance In Spite of a Poor Market, Low Interest Rates

Develop a set of comebacks you can have at your ready when prospects or donors respond negatively to your ask.

With both interest rates and the stock market at lower-than-normal levels, some development officers are facing obstacles in obtaining gifts directed toward endowment as potential contributors ask: "Why should I contribute to your endowment with interest rates being as low as they are?"

To help forge ahead, be prepared with well-thought-out comebacks to this dilemma. Here are some responses you might want to include in your comeback arsenal:

1. "Endowments go on generation after generation. Gifts to the current operating fund are important and helpful, but a gift to the endowment is a long-term investment."

2. "Although interest rates and the value of the stock market are presently low, history shows that, over time, the stock market has outperformed any investment. Some argue that the time to invest is now, when prices are cheap."

3. "We have an obligation to our organization and those we serve to ensure that our work can continue far into the future. A solid (and growing) endowment will allow us to not only survive, but thrive."

4. "Look at your own circumstances. When interest rates are low, do you simply decide to spend all your income or do you continue to try to save? It's no different with our organization. In spite of lower interest rates, we continue to believe it's important to invest in the long-term."

Why It Pays to Identify Your Prospects' Heroes

Don't assume every prospect will want an endowed fund named after him/herself. They may have a hero they wish to honor.

Take a moment and reflect: Who, outside of immediate family, are your biggest heroes? Who immediately comes to mind as someone who had a tremendously positive influence on your life? If money were no object, wouldn't you relish the opportunity to establish an endowed fund or name a building in honor or in memory of one of your heroes?

That same approach can be used as you meet with prospects capable of making significant gifts. Although many will choose to establish a gift in their own names or the name of a loved one, others will be motivated by the thought of making a gift in honor of one of their heroes.

As you meet with prospects, remember to ask probing questions that reveal their life's heroes. Who are these persons? Why do the prospects hold these individuals in such high esteem? How did their heroes help them or influence them in such momentous ways? Why might it be appropriate to tie the hero's name, in perpetuity, to the funding project you have in mind?

Don't underestimate the impact prospects' heroes can have in bringing about sizeable named gifts.

Cultivation Tactics That Play Up Prospects' Heroes

Once you have identified a prospect's hero (or heroes), use that knowledge to repeatedly build a three-way bond between the prospect, his/her hero and your institution. Here are some cultivation examples that help to accomplish that objective:

1. If you do a feature article on the prospect, point out his/her heroes and describe the influence those figures had on the life of the prospect.

2. When publicly introducing the prospect, cite one of his/her heroes, pointing out positive attributes that both individuals share.

3. If the prospect's hero is living, explore the possibility of connecting with him/her in a way the prospect would perceive as appropriate and noble — honoring the hero in some capacity, bringing the hero to your agency, etc. If the person is deceased, look at connecting with his/her family.

CULTIVATION: BUILDING THE CASE FOR SUPPORT

Actions That Recognize and Encourage Endowment Gifts

If you produce an annual report that lists all fiscal year contributors — and there are many reasons for doing so — make it a point to include a section that lists all named endowment funds. Include the names of anyone contributing to a particular fund — that year — under each respective fund name. There's more than one good reason for doing this:

1. It's a public way of thanking those who made endowment gifts during the fiscal year.

2. It lets everyone on your mailing list know that you have named endowment funds and may get them thinking about establishing a fund.

3. Those who see a named fund listed may, for one reason or another, decide to contribute to that fund.

ENDOWED FUNDS

The Susan and Thomas Kincade Scholarship Fund
- Susan and Thomas Kincade

The Martin Stanhope Landscape Fund
- Betty Stanhope
- Al and Becky Stanhope Donner

The Stoddard Corporation Endowment
- Stoddard Corporation

The Chavez Youth Camp Fund

Imagining Exercise Helps Understand Endowment's Potential

Because endowment gifts are perceived as less tangible than bricks and mortar type gifts, it helps to share regular and varied methods of educating board members about what a substantial endowment can mean to an organization.

One such example might include helping your board to understand what the nation, perhaps the world, would be like if every nonprofit in existence had a sizeable endowment that provided annual income to underwrite important programs and services. At right is such an example that you could include in a board presentation or in a letter to board members.

From time to time, conduct imagining exercises such as this with your board.

JUST IMAGINE...

It has been estimated that a nonprofit should have an endowment at least 2.5 times the size of its annual operating budget. If an agency, for instance, had an annual budget of $700,000, that would mean it should have an endowment of at least $1,750,000. Annual interest from the fund would be used to underwrite existing programs, services and costs associated with the nonprofit's operations.

Just imagine if every one of our nation's nonprofits had an endowment in place that was equal to or more than that minimum benchmark. Think about how that would impact the quality of life of our nation! Hospitals would be better able to serve those without resources. Colleges, universities and schools would be more able to expand learning opportunities. Cultural organizations would flourish. Social service agencies would be financially less dependent on government support, and able to expand services and provide greater outreach. All nonprofits would be more focused on goals aimed at thriving rather than surviving.

What a remarkable national goal — to help all nonprofits achieve minimum endowment benchmarks! Doesn't matter whether you're Republican or Democrat, male or female, African-American or Hispanic. All citizens, even our environment, would benefit. And with the future of all these worthy organizations ensured, our nation's government — at all levels (federal, state, county, city) — could focus more attention on other pressing issues.

To help achieve that lofty dream — and it is possible — let each of us make an ongoing commitment to more fully endow [Name of your organization]. I invite each of you to give thought to making a three- to five-year endowment pledge. Additionally, I ask that you consider making a plan gift that will be directed to our endowment. And finally, I ask that each of you make a concerted effort to serve as endowment ambassadors for [Name of your organization], planting endowment seeds in the minds of others and inviting them to invest in our long-term effort.

What we do now, as individual board members and collectively, will establish a precedent for others who consider making endowment investments. The legacy you establish will benefit generations to come.

CULTIVATION: BUILDING THE CASE FOR SUPPORT

Having Endowment Minimums Helps in Prospect Cultivation

Does your endowment gifts policy state that funds will be dispersed from a named fund only when the fund reaches a certain minimum level? If not, you may wish to add it to your policy. Including this information is important for two reasons:

1. It reduces endowment spending and, thus, aids in endowment growth.

2. It encourages donors to expedite their giving in order to reach the minimum dollar amount required to begin making annual awards.

    If, for example, you say that $25,000 is required to name and fund an endowed scholarship, then someone who pledges $25,000 will want to get it paid up, knowing that annual scholarships won't be awarded until that happens.

Form Provides Snapshot of Cultivation Activity

Although various forms and software allow you to track individual prospect cultivation activities — specific actions that move a prospect closer to the realization of making a major gift — the form illustrated below provides a simple snapshot of a group of prospects over a six-month period.

This prospect cultivation plan provides a way to visually compare cultivation among prospects and identify any deficits in individual prospect attention.

The form can be used by individual development officers in charge of managing a specified number of major gift prospects and it can also be used by those whose job it is to supervise development officers' cultivation activities.

The person completing the cultivation form can use this tool to plan individual cultivation strategies in advance, to keep a record of each cultivation move as it occurs and to evaluate past cultivation activity.

Simply list the names of top prospects at left and then fill in the date and type of cultivation taking place on that date — face-to-face visit (V), a visit by the prospect to your facilities (F), written correspondence (C) or phone call (P).

A simple form such as this helps to visually compare the amount and types of cultivation that has occurred among a group of prospects.

SIX-MONTH PROSPECT CULTIVATION PLAN

Prospect Manager _____

For Period Covering _____

Face-to-face visit V
Prospect visit to your facility .... F
Written correspondence C
Phone call .... P

Prospect	January	February	March	April	May	June

ADVICE ON SOLICITING AND CLOSING ENDOWMENT GIFTS

How do you determine an appropriate ask amount? What might you say to overcome a donor's objections? How can a scale of gifts help during the closing process? This chapter will help you become more accomplished at negotiating and closing endowment gifts.

How to Sell What Donors Can't See

Intangible giving options, such as an endowment, are not always the easiest to sell to potential donors, yet they are often critical to the long-term future of an organization. So, how do you sell what your donors can't see or touch?

Aggie Sweeney, CEO of the Collins Group (Seattle, WA), shares three ways to help sell donors on intangible giving options:

1. Quantify and clearly articulate the outcomes possible as a result of their gift.

2. Be able to engage the donor in the organization's work (e.g., take them on a tour of your programs).

3. Talk about what will be lost if this philanthropic investment is not made (e.g., if a social service agency, talk about lives lost; if a heritage organization, talk about the history that will be unpreserved).

"Whatever you can do to offer tangible engagement in the organization can help the donor see the value in intangible giving," she says.

Sweeney shares an example of a youth organization with whom she worked that needed to raise significant endowment funds for an environmental education program: "They took the donor and the donor's family out to a camp location, where they experienced the diversity of the environment, the shoreline and the forest, as well as seeing students involved in environmental education. Endowment is by nature a long-term investment, and with this visit the family was able to experience firsthand how they would be able to help future students learn about environmental education. The family ended up making a naming gift and helping to endow and permanently preserve that camp so that it will be available for generations to come."

Your success as a professional fundraiser will depend, in part, on your ability to help people visualize what could be.

Source: Aggie Sweeney, CEO, The Collins Group, Seattle, WA. Phone (206) 728-1755. E-mail: aggies@collinsgroup.com

Visualization represents one way to sell donors on intangible giving options, such as endowment gifts.

Scale of Gifts Helps During Closing Process

Textbook solicitation suggests that you should ask each donor for a specific gift amount when making the ask. That's true. But, there are times, for any number of legitimate reasons, where that may not be the wisest move.

In instances in which you don't feel it's right to ask for a specific amount, here's another useful approach you can take. Have a scale-of-giving chart at your disposal when it comes time for making the ask. Pull out the chart and, if you choose, use a colored marker to highlight a particular gift range or draw a circle around that portion of the gift range that you hope the prospect will come in at with a gift and then pose this question: "Where do you see yourself giving within the area I've highlighted?"

This useful method allows you to set a minimum gift level without pinpointing an exact amount.

VISIONS MADE REAL
CAMPAIGN

Goal: $8 million

Scale of Gifts Required to Achieve Goal

Gift Range	Gifts Required	Total
$1 million or more	2	$2,000,000
$500,000 to 999,999	4	$2,000,000
$250,000 to 499,999	6	$1,500,000
$100,000 to $249,999	10	$1,000,000
$50,000 to 99,999	15	$750,000
$25,000 to 49,999	20	$500,000
$10,000 to 24,999	20	$200,000
Less than $10,000	500	$50,000
		$8,000,000

ADVICE ON SOLICITING AND CLOSING ENDOWMENT GIFTS

Prepare Board Members, Volunteers for Team Solicitations

Before asking board members or other volunteers to participate in donor solicitation calls, know the roles everyone will play, says Marion Conway, principal, Marion Conway Consulting (Verona, NJ).

"Does the board member/volunteer represent the link to the potential donor as a friend, business associate or alumni of the same college, or does he or she represent an added ambassador from the organization?" Conway says. "Their role may be different depending on their relationship with the potential donor."

In either case, board members/volunteers should share with the prospect their connection with the organization and passion for its mission, their personal relationship with its work and events, how it benefits their family and the community.

Discussing major goals of the strategic plan and the vision for the organization's future is also valuable and appropriate, Conway says.

Meet in advance of the solicitation call to discuss these roles so there are no surprises at the call, she says. Cover the type of questions they will answer, and which questions you will handle: "For example, if you have developed a list of program options that the donor might support, the board member or volunteer may help figure out which options are most likely to appeal to the donor."

If the board member/volunteer has a personal relationship with the potential donor, it is appropriate for him or her to make the ask, says Conway, because it can be done in an informal and personal way. "If the board member/volunteer does not have a personal relationship with the donor, it is better for you to make the ask. In either case you should know what the specific ask will be."

Source: Marion Conway, Marion Conway Consulting, Verona, NJ. Phone (973) 239-8937. E-mail: mc@marionconwayconsulting.com

Team solicitation can be very effective as long as participants know, in advance, one another's primary roles.

Responding to Prospect's Comment: 'That's a Lot of Money!'

You've been cultivating a major gift prospect for nearly 18 months. You know of one instance in which she has made a $100,000 gift to another charity, but you also believe she's capable of giving much more than that. Together, you have determined her funding interests, but no dollar figure has been discussed. Today's the big day: You present her with a proposal for a $350,000 gift. She glances at it, notices the dollar amount and, in amazement, says: "That's a lot of money!"

How do you respond at that moment? What can you possibly say? Here are some options:

1. **Wait for the prospect's next comment before saying anything.** Silence can be deadly, but it can also be wise to wait for a follow-up comment. Although the prospect could say "that's too much for me to give," she may also make a more hopeful response: "It is a lot of money, but I guess it's not out of the realm of possibility."

2. **Be prepared to negotiate.** Respond with a comment such as: "Yes, that is a very generous investment, but please keep in mind that it could be given over a period of time."

3. **Emphasize the gift's impact and its benefits.** "Not only will the annual interest from this endowed fund benefit some 20 children each year, the named fund will be a lasting tribute in honor of your parents for generations to come."

It pays to anticipate donor objections in advance.

Tips for Making the Ask

- Be specific in asking for a dollar amount. If possible, avoid presenting a gift range.
- Present the prospect with a written proposal. This makes it clear that your request is formal and implies that a formal response is needed.

Remember the Four Rs

Here's a long-standing development axiom that's worth repeating: A major gift results from 1) the right solicitor, 2) asking for the right amount, 3) for the right purpose, 4) at the right time.

ADVICE ON SOLICITING AND CLOSING ENDOWMENT GIFTS

Written Proposals Need Not Be for Solicitation Only

Some development professionals may think the only time you should submit a gift proposal is when you're about to make the ask. Not so. Written proposals need not be for solicitation purposes only; they can also be a way to get a prospect thinking more seriously about a gift.

How a proposal is perceived depends, in part, on how it is presented to a prospect and the language used throughout it. Consider prefacing a written proposal with: "I'm sharing this proposal with you today, not to get an answer one way or the other, but to use as a discussion tool, as a way for us to explore your funding interests...." The prospect will feel less pressured to give an acceptance or rejection to your proposal.

Also, if the document's wording sets a tone of exploring the possibilities rather than seeking a "yes" or "no" response, the recipient of the document will approach your proposal with a more open mind.

Below is an example of a one-page proposal intended as an exploratory tool rather than an outright solicitation. Note how the language of this example is more subtle in its approach than an outright ask for a major gift would be.

Don't limit written proposals to solicitation purposes only. They can also be beneficial in getting a prospect to seriously consider a gift.

An Exploratory Proposal
Prepared Especially for

JOHN AND MILDRED SAUNDERS

Preface: It is not our intent to ask you for a major gift commitment at this time. Rather, the purpose of this proposal is to help us, together, explore your interests in XYZ Medical Center based on our funding needs at this time. We have outlined several possible funding opportunities which we can discuss. Should you develop a particular interest in one of these options, we can provide one or more follow-up proposals that will include greater detail.

As you consider these various funding interests, please give thought to possible naming options as well. A naming gift could bear your names or the names of anyone else you choose — a family member, a mentor, a historic figure, etc.

Naming Gift Options

Maintenance and Enhancement Endowments — Annual interest from an endowed fund would be used to maintain and/or enhance any of these existing programs or facilities or equipment. The degree to which an annual fund would go beyond maintenance and be used for enhancement would be determined by the size of the fund.

- Nursing — Professional Development
- Surgery Center
- Cancer Center
- Obstetrics
- Burn and Poison Center
- Landscaping and Grounds
- Equipment Maintenance Fund

New Initiatives Endowments — None of the following funds presently exist at XYZ Medical Center. Naming funds directed to any of these programs or improvements would enhance our services and our reputation as one of the premier health organizations throughout the region.

- Nursing Education Scholarship Funds — Directed to nursing students who agree to serve our hospital for a minimum number of years after receiving their degrees.

- Good Samaritan Fund — To assist in underwriting the medical costs of financially deserving patients.

- Equipment Acquisitions Fund — Annual interest from this equipment endowment would be used to purchase equipment not presently available to XYZ Medical Center.

ADVICE ON SOLICITING AND CLOSING ENDOWMENT GIFTS

Endowment Formula

Use this formula as one guide in determining the size of the endowment you would need for a particular project:

The size of the gift needed should equal the amount needed annually for the donor's purpose, divided by the endowment payout rate. This formula is rough, however, especially if you are using a rolling multiyear average upon which the payout rate percentage is applied.

Prepare, Practice to Better Handle Donor Objections

Before you make that all-important face-to-face ask of a major donor, be sure you do your homework to ensure that the donor is both willing to support the project and capable of making a gift in the amount of your ask, says John H. Taylor, associate vice chancellor of advancement services, North Carolina State University (Raleigh, NC).

"The number of donor objections will be low if you've done your homework," says Taylor, "including researching the donor's giving history to your organization and to similar organizations, and matching the donor's interests with your needs."

Objections do happen, however, even with the most careful research and cultivation of a donor. The fundraising expert shares some of the situations in which a donor might object to making a major gift and how to handle those objections:

"My financial situation has changed."

If you have not met with the donor for some time, you may not be aware of a change in the donor's financial situation. If the donor tells you that his or her financial situation has changed, the best and most appropriate response is to talk about payment options. For example, you can say that you are not talking about the donor making a $1 million gift today, but instead making a gift of $250,000 a year over a period of four years. If the donor still objects, you may have to put it on the back burner and come back to the donor at a later date.

"That project doesn't interest me."

This objection shouldn't happen very often if you have done your research, but in case you've picked the wrong project for the donor, you should always go into the solicitation with multiple gift options. "Although you will want to go in with a primary focus, you don't want to go in with only one choice or you will either have to go back to them later with a revised project, or fumble around with other ideas in front of the donor," he says. "It's better to go in with two to three viable options and let the donor pick the one of greatest interest to him or her."

"Something happened at your organization recently that I'm not happy with."

You may have made the solicitation appointment six months ago, and in the interim, something has happened at your organization that has made your donor mad. "For example, your organization may have had some negative publicity that affected the donor's personal beliefs," Taylor says. "You will want to look introspectively at what has gone on at your organization between the time you made the appointment and the time of the solicitation to make sure nothing has happened. If it has, and you think your donor might be offended, you might want to reschedule your solicitation appointment until you can work out the problem with your donor."

Source: John H. Taylor, Associate Vice Chancellor, Advancement Services, North Carolina State University, Raleigh, NC. Phone (919) 513-2954. E-mail: johnhtaylor@ncsu.edu

Methods for Determining Ask Amount

Various rules of thumb serve as guides in setting an appropriate ask amount. Keep in mind, however, these are intended as guides only. Having said that, here is one method for determining the ask amount based on a five-year pledge period:

Here's one method to consider when determining an appropriate ask amount.

Take the individual's average yearly contribution and multiply that by 20. If, for instance, someone was contributing $1,000 on an annual basis, you would take that number times 20 to get the ask amount of $20,000. Because this is for a capital campaign that seeks a higher level of sacrificial giving, the request is based on an ask that is four times the donor's annual gift to be given annually for five years (4 x $1,000 x 5 years gives you $20,000).

You may choose to increase or decrease that sacrificial multiplier — in this example, 4 — depending on the prospect's financial capability and proclivity to give.

ADVICE ON SOLICITING AND CLOSING ENDOWMENT GIFTS

Expert Advice Will Help You Turn Donor Objections Into Gift Opportunities

Before you can turn donor objections into opportunities, you must first realize one key concept, according to Sandra Ehrlich, director of fund development services, and Dawn M.S. Miller, senior consultant, Zielinksi Companies (St. Louis, MO): Fundraising is sharing what you believe in such as way that you offer your donors an opportunity to participate with you in your mission, core values and vision.

"A donor objection is truly a window of opportunity for the solicitor to listen and draw the donor closer to his or her mission," says Ehrlich. "Giving is based on the wants and needs of the donor. Therefore, your role is to help the donor visualize the result the gift will make to the greater community by overcoming their objections."

Studies show the oral presentation is ultimately what motivates donors to make the gift, the fundraising experts say. Through philanthropic storytelling, you inspire and motivate donors by sharing the urgency, importance and relevance of their gifts.

"When soliciting major gifts one-on-one, it is vital to listen and watch for those nonverbal cues and clues that make up roughly 85 percent of the conversation," says Miller. "At the same time, listen for 'gifting noises' and donor objections that demonstrate how deeply the donor cares about your mission."

Before a solicitation meeting, they advise, role-play situations and ask a series of questions to uncover and overcome objections. Remember to restate donor questions and objections, and identify when the donor is listening or he/she is shutting down.

"Hank Rosso, founder of The Fundraising School in San Francisco, said that there are six 'right' considerations in the gift solicitation process to maximize fundraising success," says Miller. "They are: the right person asks the right prospect for the right amount of money for the right cause at the right time and in the right way."

To overcome objections, say Ehrlich and Miller, you will need to objectively listen for and determine the answers to these six key questions:

1. Am I the right solicitor, or natural partner, for this donor?
2. Is this a philanthropic "fit" for the donor? Is this one of his/her top three priorities?
3. Is it the amount we're asking?
4. Is it the organization? The project? The program? Is it who we are serving?
5. Is it the right time for the donor to make a gift of this magnitude?
6. What would the donor like to support? How would the donor like to make the gift?

"By closely examining what the donor is saying, and perhaps more importantly, not saying, you can turn the donor's objections into a gift," says Ehrlich.

Sources: Sandra G. Ehrlich, Director of Fund Development Services, and Dawn M.S. Miller, Senior Consultant, Zielinski Companies, St. Louis, MO. Phone (800) 489-2150; (314) 644-2150. E-mail: ehrlich@zielinskico.com or dmiller@zielinskico.com

Content not available in this edition

Be Prepared to Answer Common Gift Objections

Don't take no for an answer when soliciting a donor for a major gift. Sandra Ehrlich, director of fund development services, and Dawn M.S. Miller, senior consultant, Zielinski Companies (St. Louis, MO), share their answers to 10 common donor gift objections:

1. The donor says: "I just don't know." You say: "What are your concerns?"

2. The donor says: "I can't make up my mind." You say: "What have I left unclear?"

3. The donor says: "I'm not ready to give." You say: "When would be a good time?"

4. The donor says: "No." You say: "May I ask why?" (Remember, "no" is not usually forever — is "no" right now?)

5. The donor says: "Your request is too high." You say: "In respect to what?"

6. The donor says: "I'd like to help, but that figure is way out of my range." You say: "What would you feel comfortable giving at this time?"

7. The donor says: "I don't have enough money." Or, "I'm going to retire in a few years." You say: "What if I can show you a way to make a gift?"

8. The donor says: "I have to talk to my husband/wife first." You say: "When would it be convenient for us to talk together?"

9. The donor says: "I need to make sure my spouse is provided for." You say: "What if we talk about gift plans that may help you provide income for your spouse and support our organization too?"

10. The donor says: "I don't give lump sums." Or, "I don't make pledges." You say: "How would you prefer to give?" or "What would work better for you?"

ADVICE ON SOLICITING AND CLOSING ENDOWMENT GIFTS

Endowment Questionnaire Helps Support Relationship With Donor

Fred A. Matthews, senior advisor, Matthews Philanthropic Strategies (Issaquah, WA), has developed a brief questionnaire development staff use to help clarify a donor's intentions and preferences related to a proposed endowment fund before an endowment agreement is signed.

To clarify a donor's endowment preferences, consider using a questionnaire such as the example shown here.

"The purpose of the questionnaire is to establish up front some of the important matters related to the endowment so they can be incorporated into the endowment agreement," Matthews says. "All too often, some of these matters are not discussed or included in the agreement and can come back to haunt the organization and potentially sour the relationship with the donor or the heirs."

With information gleaned from this questionnaire, Matthews says, organizations will be in a strong position to have the endowment agreement include key matters the donor and the organization need to know and accept. "By doing this, the implementation of the endowment and the relationship with the donor should be smooth and rewarding for both parties," he says.

Plus, he says, the questionnaire can help development staff avoid these four pitfalls:

1. Confusion between the donor and organization about how the gift will be used.

2. Accepting a gift for a purpose the organization cannot use or that is not program-related.

3. Developing a relationship with the family through a memorial or honor gift and missing the opportunity related to heirs after the death of the donor.

4. Having the donor(s) assume that he/she/they will have a guiding role in how the endowment is spent.

Source: Fred A. Matthews, Senior Advisor, Matthews Philanthropic Strategies, Issaquah, WA. Phone (425) 313-0987. E-mail: fredamatthews@msn.com

Content not available in this edition

ADVICE ON SOLICITING AND CLOSING ENDOWMENT GIFTS

Include an Executive Summary With All Proposals

Do you follow a standard outline when crafting major gift proposals? Whether you do or not, make a point to include an executive summary at the beginning of your written document. The reason for that is twofold:

1. If written properly, a proposal summary will tempt the potential donor to read on. As you draft the summary, view it through the eyes of the would-be donor. In 200 words or less, what can you say that will captivate the reader? Obviously, the proposed name of the fund or building project will draw attention. The way you describe the impact of the donor's gift may also come into play. If the donor has an obvious interest in the future growth of a proposed endowment fund or the annual interest from it, for instance, you may want to devote more words to the way the gift will be invested and how it relates to your overall endowment.

2. Summaries will also help to ensure readers see the document's big picture if they choose to read no further. Knowing that could happen, the summary should include the ask amount, what the realization of that gift would accomplish, and the benefits to the donor for making that gift a reality. Do not include the payout period for your request; that's an item that can be negotiated as the gift is finalized.

Sample executive summary for a proposed endowment gift.

EXECUTIVE SUMMARY

The creation of the Samuel and LaDonna Stallings Endowment Fund — based on a $1 million gift from you, Mr. and Mrs. Stallings — will impact The Girls' Club of Saratoga like no other gift in the history of this organization.

Yours will be a transformational gift — one that allows The Girls' Club of Saratoga to bring new and improved services to more clients than any Girls' Club throughout the nation has ever been able to provide. Thanks to your hoped-for generosity, our local Girls' Club of Saratoga will become a model for other female youth agencies throughout the nation.

Annual interest from the fund, based on a 6-percent return, will provide $60,000 each year which will be used to benefit some 500 girls who utilize our services each year, underwriting programs such as our After School Program, Families Together, Young Women Mentors Program and more. In addition, annual income from your fund will be used to attract and compensate only the most highly skilled and talented staff.

The realization of this gift will also raise the sights of others associated with The Girls' Club of Saratoga, encouraging them to consider what they might be capable of doing to improve the lives of young women through their investment in our cause.

Mr. and Mrs. Stallings, you hold the key to unlocking a boundless and exciting future for the young women of our community — one that other communities throughout our nation will want to emulate. Your transformational gift will provide an abundance of nurturing for young women of this region for generations to come.

We look forward to exploring this with both of you. Thank you for your positive consideration.

Be Sure About Endowment Gift Designation

When you ask a prospect for a gift to your organization's endowment, that means the principal will never be touched; only the annual interest. Right?

Wrong! Some nonprofits will raise gifts under the umbrella of endowment but book them as quasi-endowment. Under that designation, such gifts can be used for purposes other than endowment, if necessary.

As a key solicitor of funds, you need to be fully aware of how endowment gifts are being designated so you can be totally up front with prospects considering a major gift to your endowment. The majority of persons who make endowment gifts assume that the corpus will never be touched.

ADVICE ON SOLICITING AND CLOSING ENDOWMENT GIFTS

Include Examples in Endowment Proposals

In preparing a written proposal for an endowment gift, make a point to share one or more examples of similar endowment funds at your institution. Even if you choose not to share the names of particular funds, quantitatively and qualitatively illustrate how those funds are making a positive difference for your organization and for those you serve.

Referencing the impact endowments have had and are making among those you serve will help donors and would-be donors visualize what their gifts can and will accomplish.

If you're going after an endowed scholarship, for example, reference the number of students an existing scholarship has helped over its lifetime. How many awards have been made? What's the total dollar amount that was awarded since its inception? In addition to helping students, how has the scholarship helped your institution?

Those real-life examples help would-be donors visualize the long-term value of an endowed gift.

> **Pingrey Endowed Scholarship Fund**
>
> Established: 1993
> Total number of recipients since inception: 28
> Average scholarship amount: $2,500
> Total award amount since inception: $70,000
> Sampling of recipients' careers since graduation:
>
> 1 Pediatrician
> 2 Sales executives with Fortune 500 companies
> 1 Priest
> 2 Nurses
> 3 Entrepreneurs
>
> Worth noting: 100 percent of all past recipients are supporting the college and four recipients have established endowed funds.

Work at Improving Your Negotiation Skills

Knowing when and how to negotiate is both an art and a science. Many successful solicitations are the result of appropriately timed and thought-out negotiations.

Here are three techniques that can help you become a better negotiator:

It's important to recognize what can be negotiated during the solicitation phase.

1. Determine your position in advance of your appointment and attempt to anticipate the prospect's possible reactions so you will be prepared with counter offers.

2. Don't get so hung up on details that you lose sight of your primary objective. If, for instance, the prospect prefers to pay your requested amount over a five-year period rather than two years, be prepared to accept those conditions.

3. Pay attention to what is motivating the donor. It pays to listen. Be sensitive to what is motivating the potential gift, and use that information to close your sale. If the prospect is driven by ego, for instance, focus on those donor benefits.

Simple Endowment Proposal Serves as Catalyst

If your organization has had little experience raising major gifts for endowment, don't let that stop you from pursuing them. After all, don't need a 100-page proposal to land big gifts. Often, a simple two- or three-page proposal is sufficient to spark the interest of a new donor.

Here's a format you can follow to customize your own proposal:

> ### Rule of Thumb
>
> - While this rule has many exceptions, it generally takes anywhere from 18 to 24 months of active cultivation before a relationship with a prospect is mature enough to ask for a gift.

Part 1 — Title page: "The John and Mary Doe Endowed Scholarship." Selecting both a name and purpose for an endowment gift often provides the fuel that gets prospects imagining what it would be like to make a naming gift and how it could be used.

Part 2 — Mechanics of an endowed gift. Explain how the principal would be invested and annual interest used for intended programs for generations to come.

Part 3 — Description of the proposed endowed gift's use. Help prospects visualize how their gifts would positively impact your organization and those you serve.

Part 4 — Spell out benefits to the donor.

ADVICE ON SOLICITING AND CLOSING ENDOWMENT GIFTS

Craft a Gift Agreement Spelling Out Donor's Wishes

A gift agreement that addresses the interests of both the donor and the charity will provide lasting clarity to both and pave the way for possible additional major gift commitments.

Some gift agreements — often referred to as letters of intent — spell out the terms of a major gift. In doing so, they often benefit the charity more than the donor. Such gift agreements typically identify key points such as:

- Total pledge amount.
- Pledge payout period — how often gifts will be made and for how much.
- Timing of payments — when they are to be made.
- Intended use of the gift.
- Gift type — cash, equities, land, etc.

As vital as a letter of intent is when accepting a major gift pledge, it is equally important — for the donor's sake — to develop a gift agreement that takes the donor's wishes into account, as well. Whether in the letter of intent or part of a separate document, it's important that certain issues be addressed for the sake of the donor.

While it's true that such a document helps protect the charity as well as the donor, it's simply good stewardship to look out for the best interests of the donor.

This particular example addresses issues such as:

- What is donor's purpose in making the gift? What specifically does he/she want it to accomplish?
- How much publicity does donor want? Or does he/she want total anonymity?
- Does donor have special conditions attached to the gift? Some donors, for instance, insist on a provision in the event the charity dissolves.

To ensure your donor's wishes are fulfilled, consider drafting a gift agreement that spells out the terms of the gift.

This sample gift agreement shows how such a form can emphasize a donor's wishes and take the charity's issues into consideration.

Content not available in this edition

Negotiating the Pledge

- If a prospect has just said he will pledge $150,000 over a three-year period but you were hoping for more, ask if it would help to maximize his ability to do more by extending the payout period for another two years. At $50,000 per year, that would result in another $100,000.

ADVICE ON SOLICITING AND CLOSING ENDOWMENT GIFTS

Be Prepared for Endowed Gift With an Official Endowment Agreement

What's your procedure for accepting endowment gifts? Do you have an agreement form that spells out details of the pledge and the way in which annual income will be used?

Staff at one Northeast public radio station created a written endowment agreement after receiving a $1 million endowment gift, the station's first gift of that size.

For example, because this recipient was a public radio station and the staff was unsure how its programs may change in the future, they created the agreement to allow them more flexibility while still meeting the donor's wishes.

Section 5 of the agreement, for instance, clearly spells out that the funds will be used for the purpose the donor intended as long as the radio station continues to offer that programming. If at any time that programming changes, the radio station must contact the donor or trustee of the donor's estate to discuss how the money could be used in the station's new capacity.

While part of the contents of the endowment agreement can carry over into future agreements as boilerplate language, certain aspects will change to reflect the donor's wishes as well as the purpose of the gift.

Content not available in this edition

Explain Endowment Gift Impact

When soliciting or making the case for an endowment gift, quantify how it will impact your organization and those you serve:

"An endowment gift of $500,000, even based on a yearly return of only 3 percent, would provide $15,000 in new computer purchases and maintenance each year. At today's prices, we could purchase 10 to 15 new computers yearly, ensuring that every child in our community has an opportunity to gain computer literacy at a young age."

Endowment Builder: Practical Ideas for Securing Endowment Gifts, Second Edition.
Edited by Scott C. Stevenson.
© 2009 Stevenson, Inc. Published 2009 by Stevenson, Inc.

STARTING AND ADDING TO NAMED ENDOWMENTS

How might you introduce the idea of a named endowment fund? How do you determine thresholds for named funds? There's no doubt that naming a fund plays a significant role in motivating major gifts. It enables far greater ownership by the donor and even encourages subsequent gifts to the named fund.

Study Named Endowments to Forecast Campaign Gifts

If you're planning a capital campaign that includes an endowment component, be sure to review all existing named endowment funds as one component of your overall goal-setting procedures.

Because existing endowment donors will be among your best prospects for future endowment gifts, it makes sense to estimate potential endowment gifts from those sources. Many of those current donors will look favorably at adding to their existing endowments, while simultaneously participating in your campaign.

Estimate what each donor might be willing to add to his/her existing endowment fund as part of a campaign pledge to be paid out over a one- to five-year period. Also, if your campaign will include irrevocable planned gifts, some donors may choose to make a planned gift as well (or in lieu of an outright gift).

Trying to get an idea of where you campaign's gifts will come from and how much you might expect from each source? Analyze your existing named endowments to estimate gift potential from these sources.

Celebrate the Activation of a Named Fund

Seven years ago, a donor pledged $25,000 to establish a named endowment fund at your organization. The final payment is coming up, and the fund will soon kick in. How will you mark the occasion?

Donors often wait several years — until the fund reaches a certain level — before witnessing the fruits of their investments. Make a point to celebrate when a named endowment fund activates. Invite the donor to your premises to show what fund proceeds will accomplish. Provide a written summary of the fund's impact for the first year. Above all, recognize the culmination of their efforts when the day finally arrives!

Offer Varying Endowment Thresholds

The amount of money required to establish a named endowment should be determined by what that fund will be expected to accomplish and the visibility the fund will generate in relation to other funds.

Your nonprofit's age, constituency size and historical giving will also play into setting threshold amounts for various types of endowments.

The key is to offer a variety of endowment opportunities with varying thresholds to give everyone a choice. Not everyone can afford to endow a faculty chair with a threshold of $1 million, nor does a faculty chair appeal to everyone.

Develop a menu of naming endowment opportunities, such as the example shown here, to include in handouts and promote on your website.

Named Endowment Opportunities

This is a sampling of naming gift endowments you can establish. Minimum gift levels to create various types of endowments have been set to guarantee income will be adequate to achieve the benefactor's vision, now and in the future. Gifts may be added later to build the endowment over time.

Endowment Type	Threshold Required
Building	$5,000,000*
Departmental Endowment	$3,000,000
Chair	$1,000,000
Lectureship	$500,000
Equipment Fund	$500,000
Visiting Professor	$250,000
Program Endowment	$100,000*
Office Endowment	$50,000*
Book Fund	$25,000
Internship	$25,000
Recognition Award/Prize	$25,000
Scholarship	$25,000
Auditorium Seating	$5,000 *Thresholds Vary*

Endowments may be established with less than threshold amounts; however, the threshold should be reached within a reasonable time.

Share a variety of endowment opportunities with new prospects as a starting point.

STARTING AND ADDING TO NAMED ENDOWMENTS

Help Donors Decide What to Call Named Gifts

Share a naming considerations form with endowment donors to help them select their top naming choice.

How much support do you offer donors as they weigh what to call a newly endowed scholarship, a newly launched program or renovated space in a building? Do you simply throw out a couple of possibilities or do you guide them through a process that will make them more fully satisfied with their final decision?

Make use of a naming considerations form (such as the one shown below) that can aid donors in selecting their top choice for a named gift. Meet with those involved to point out various naming possibilities, then encourage them to take some time to weigh those possibilities before making a final decision.

Naming Considerations Form

As you weigh naming possibilities for your gift, recognize the many choices that are available to you. Your gift could be named in honor/memory of:

❑ Parent   ❑ Mentor   ❑ Yourself
❑ Child   ❑ Business   ❑ Spouse
❑ Other Family   ❑ Business Associate   ❑ A Place
❑ Other _____

Once you have selected a name (or combination of names), give thought to the manner in which you would prefer to have the name(s) listed:

Last name only:	The Walsh Fund
Combination of names:	The Michael and Kate Walsh Fund
	The Walsh/Lester Fund
Inclusion of maiden names:	The Susan Shaw Walsh Fund
Inclusion of "memorial":	The Albert Walsh Memorial Fund
Descriptive wording:	The Walsh Scholarship Fund
	Walsh Family Seminar Room

Write down naming possibilities that come to mind in the first column, then prioritize your choices in the second column:

1. _____   1. _____
2. _____   2. _____
3. _____   3. _____
4. _____   4. _____
5. _____   5. _____
6. _____   6. _____
7. _____   7. _____
8. _____   8. _____

Susan Elston Endowment Fund

Date	Contribution Amounts
11/21/00	$5,000
11/02/01	$2,500
11/22/02	$3,000
2003	—
2004	—
5/05/05	$2,500
9/07/06	$2,500
10/10/07	$8,000
10/11/08	$8,000
9/21/09	$3,500
Fund Total	$35,000

Point Out Past Contributions

What are you doing to encourage donors who have named endowment funds to add to those funds regularly? Here's one action you should take:

Once each year, even if a donor hasn't made a contribution to his/her endowment fund that year, provide a written report that illustrates the fund's total along with what has been given each year since the fund's inception. Doing so is not only a good stewardship practice but also serves as a visual reminder of what has (or hasn't) been done to make the named fund grow in recent years.

It's like reviewing your personal savings account information. You're more likely to add to it if you periodically review your history of deposits.

STARTING AND ADDING TO NAMED ENDOWMENTS

Urge Named Endowment Donors to Add to Funds

Officials with one Midwest historical society proactively encourage named endowment fund donors to add to their funds — with impressive results.

In a seven-year time span, the society's named endowment funds increased from 23 to 66, and the society went from no pooled named endowment funds to nine. The organization's deferred gift portfolio grew from 22 to 113 provisions, 48 of which have a combined estimated value of $8.5 million. Also in that time, the society's identified prospects grew in number from 30 to 876.

Four major methods were used by society officials to encourage this:

1. Having donors start the fund with a cash gift and supplement it with a deferred gift (typically a will provision), which allows donors to see the fund's benefits in their lifetime.

2. Sending donors annual endowed fund reports to build confidence and affinity for the fund. Reports include cover letters detailing fund performance and stating what program areas benefited from the fund in the last year. The program person will also typically write a letter to represent the fund's recipients.

3. Asking for an additional gift after appropriate cultivation.

4. Showing donors the valuable work and additional need of the program area/historic site the fund benefits, typically with visits/staff contact.

Visual Encourages Endowment Donors to Add to Funds

What are you doing to encourage existing endowment donors to add to their named funds? Unless you have been instructed differently, these special donors should be invited to add to their funds periodically by making both outright and planned gifts.

To vary your presentation style and to help them visually understand the value of additional contributions to an existing fund, make use of an endowment projection chart (like the one below) that can be tailored to their specific fund. The chart shows a donor how gift additions in particular amounts would translate into accomplishing more of what the fund was designed to do (e.g., more scholarship funding, more dollars for acquisitions, additional budget to expand or enhance a program, etc.).

When sharing an endowment project chart with a donor, you will need to decide whether it shows both outright and planned gift illustrations or only one of the two, depending on that donor's circumstances. For example, you may choose to share a chart on one occasion that illustrates only outright gift additions, and then two years later, offer a chart that has both outright and planned gift additions.

Help give donors an idea of how additional gifts to their named funds would translate into accomplishing more for your nonprofit.

John and Mary Doe Landscape Enhancement Fund
Endowment Projection Chart

Current Fund $125,000   As of May 2009

Presently, the John and Mary Doe Landscape Enhancement Fund provides $6,250 in yearly funds — based on an average 5-percent return — to maintain and enhance the Center's outdoor environment. Since the fund was established four years ago, we have been able to:

1. Redo major walkways around the grounds.
2. Add a fountain and garden on the south side of the Center.
3. Plant limited amounts of shrubbery and annuals at key locations.

These improvements have improved the sightliness of our grounds and have been positively noticed by visitors time and again.

To accomplish even more enhancements to our outdoor environment, we respectfully invite you to consider adding to this fund at this time. To help illustrate what endowment increases would accomplish, the following chart has been prepared:

Additional Gift	Total Fund	Annual Income Available
$ 250,000	$375,000	$18,750
$ 150,000	$275,000	$13,750
$ 75,000	$200,000	$10,000

STARTING AND ADDING TO NAMED ENDOWMENTS

Create a Model Room to Promote Naming Gifts

Give donors and prospective donors a sneak peek at what could-be if they were to endow a particular project (e.g., a patient or dorm room).

If one or more of your organization's buildings includes several similar types of rooms — classrooms, patient rooms, offices, etc. — a great gift opportunity lies before you. Why not create a model room and use that as a way to promoting named room opportunities?

Having a model room complete with all of the amenities — new furnishings, carpeting, lighting, updated technology, etc. — allows you to show them the before-and-after effect and help them visualize what their named room would look like. In fact, find one donor who will cover the cost of that first model room.

How much should it cost to name a room? Figure in all costs associated with renovating the existing room and then add a sufficient amount to cover future maintenance costs by endowing the room.

The Science of Setting a Building's Price Tag

Setting an appropriate gift amount to name a building can depend on various factors: location, the building's size and perceived importance and more. The cost of endowing that facility — to cover upkeep and maintenance — should also be a key consideration.

When considering what price to place on a naming opportunity for a new or existing facility, begin by looking at what other benchmark nonprofits are requiring for naming opportunities and what your market can bear.

Before an amount is decided upon, several discussions need to take place between your CEO and key advancement staff members. Once agreement is reached, your board needs to buy into and approve the decision. That board-approved decision should then become a part of your organization's naming gifts policy.

This policy should clarify any questions or issues that may arise. For example, if a significant portion of a building is to be funded through private gifts, you may decide on a minimum percent required to name the facility. If the building cost is $15 million, for instance, and 50 percent of the cost is required to name the facility, the naming gift must be $7.5 million.

> **Rule of Thumb**
>
> As one of many guidelines you can use, figure that one-half to one-third of the cost of a building project is needed as a private gift to name it.

And if an entire building is being paid for with state funds, the naming gift should be set at a much lower amount. Those naming gift funds won't be used to pay for bricks and mortar projects, but can be placed into an endowment to cover future maintenance costs and to benefit the programs housed in the facility. Also, these minimum naming percentages can be adjusted upward or downward depending on the location and prestige of the building, along with other factors.

Naming Policy Considerations

Here are some of the considerations that your naming gifts policy should address:

- ✓ Size of a gift required to name a physical space or endowed fund.
- ✓ Requirement of establishing an endowment to support the overhead and maintenance of the named facility.
- ✓ Availability of existing spaces that have never been named.
- ✓ How to address already named spaces and facilities that will be demolished or renovated.
- ✓ Whether the naming of a building or an area requires a completed gift agreement and receipt of cash or assets that can be converted to cash immediately.
- ✓ Whether buildings will be named in honor of a donor in return for an estate commitment.
- ✓ The design, wording and placement of plaques that recognize donors.
- ✓ The appropriateness of naming spaces, facilities, endowments or programs based on extraordinary service rather than a particular gift amount.

STARTING AND ADDING TO NAMED ENDOWMENTS

Using Back Door Solicitation May Be Appropriate at Times

One sales technique that has been used during the solicitation process is known as the assumptive close. With this method, the solicitor assumes the prospect will be making a major gift and, instead of making an outright ask, focuses on one or more details associated with the assumed gift.

If, for instance, the prospect has shown interest in establishing an endowed fund, discuss what such a fund would be called (as illustrated at right). Focusing in on what the donor would like to call his/her fund assumes there will be a forthcoming gift.

Naming Possibilities
for an Endowed Gift from
John and Elizabeth Widdlesey

The following naming fund possibilities are intended to assist you in selecting a name for your endowment fund. You may also want to consider naming the fund in memory or in honor of a loved one, a respected associate or even a historic figure.

A. The John and Elizabeth Widdlesey Endowed Fund

B. The John Widdlesey Endowment and The Elizabeth Widdlesey Endowment (two separate funds)

C. The Widdlesey Family Fund

D. The Widdlesey Achievement Fund

E. The Widdlesey Recognition Fund

F. The Widdlesey Scholarship Fund

G. Additional Possibilities _____

_____

Help Prospects Explore Various Naming Possibilities

As you work with prospects on various funding projects, it will be helpful to illustrate a wide variety of naming gift possibilities so they can select one that best meets their goals and desires.

Beyond using the donor's own name, he/she can choose from among these "in honor" or "in memory" possibilities:

- Parents of the donor
- Grandparents of the donor
- Donor's spouse
- Company name
- Mentor
- National hero
- Children of the donor
- Name combination (e.g., Smith/Harken)
- Religious figure
- Celebrity or public servant
- Community, state or regional name: The Dallas Center
- Someone associated with your charity: founding member, respected employee
- Someone served by your organization: former patient, victim, student

Consider Less Pricey Naming Gifts, Too

As much as we would prefer all million-dollar naming gifts, there are reasons why you should offer far less expensive naming gifts as well. A $1,000 naming gift from a non-donor, for example, may be what's necessary to establish a relationship with a new donor. And that relationship may turn into a larger naming gift down the road.

Here are some inexpensive naming gift opportunities that could run anywhere from $100 to $10,000:

- Bricks in the walkway or wall.
- Seats (theater, auditorium).
- Rooms (residence hall, patient rooms).
- Desks, computers and more.

Look for Imaginative Naming Gifts

Always maintain a list of naming gift opportunities — even when you're not in a capital campaign. Your wish list of naming opportunities should include a wide range of gift amounts and gift uses.

Be creative in identifying what might be appropriate for your cause. Consider these and other naming gift possibilities:

- Individual trees on your premises.
- An atrium or lobby area.
- A private street or access road on your premises.
- Individually endowed parking spaces.
- A supplies acquisition fund.
- A professional development fund for support staff.
- Scholarships for senior citizens.
- A volunteer work room.
- Special outdoor spaces: hiking/biking trail, tennis courts, mall area.
- Programs: wellness, mentor, travel, outreach.
- An aviary.
- Special rooms: dining room, game room, conference room.
- Positions: visiting lecturer, CEO, chaplain, docent, researcher.

Timing and Tact Are Key to Establishing Named Memorials

Don't underestimate the importance of exploring major gift opportunities — or at least planting the seed — during the loss of a loved one.

Although it's important to use a great deal of tact in determining if and when you should broach the subject of a memorial with the deceased's loved ones, it is very appropriate to at least outline the options available when family members come to you or publicly announce that memorial gifts may be directed to your charity. When that does occur, follow these guidelines:

Whenever an individual or family names your organization the recipient of memorial gifts, don't overlook the possibility of the family establishing a named endowment fund as a more lasting legacy.

1. **Cover procedures for handling memorial gifts as soon as you are notified.** Explain that all memorial gifts directed to your charity will be placed in a holding account until a later date when you and the appropriate family member(s) can meet to determine how the gifts will be used. Also inform the family that, in addition to sending donors a note of thanks, the names, addresses and gift amounts of all contributors will be given to the family.

2. **Be sure your charity is well represented at the funeral and/or wake.** If your charity has been or might be named a recipient of memorial gifts, it's only appropriate that your presence is obvious. You might even want to provide flowers or a plant.

3. **Follow up within days.** Depending on the circumstances and the wishes of family members, set an appointment to meet and review memorial possibilities. Have a standard presentation developed — such as the example at left — to outline gift possibilities.

Memorial Gift Options

<u>If memorial gifts amount to less than $1,000</u>
Have a prepared wish list of needs — perhaps identified by your development committee — with attached dollar amounts. Include a range of dollar amounts and uses. This allows families to decide on the exact use of memorial funds without simply having funds disappear into your organization's annual budget.

Explain that the memorial — plus the names of all who contributed — will be listed in your organization's annual report of contributors.

<u>For memorial gifts between $1,000 and $10,000</u>
Once again, share a wish list of needs, only this time identify more significant needs that include naming opportunities based on the overall amount contributed toward the memorial. Memorial gifts totaling $2,000, for instance, could be used to name an item — a flowing water fountain or a meeting room table — while a gift of $9,000 might name an office or a particular room in honor of someone.

<u>For memorial gifts that may amount to $10,000 or more</u>
Gifts totaling $10,000 or more — even if given by family members over a period of years (or through a bequest) — could be used to establish various types of named endowment funds or to name even more significant physical projects (e.g., The Alice Riley Cancer Center, The Mark Steffenson Reading Room). Once again, it's helpful to have an identified list of needs. With this level of giving, however, it's important that the donor have some say in shaping the exact use of the gift so he/she develops a greater sense of ownership.

Sample memorial presentation to be used with family members of the deceased.

Become Familiar With Reasons For Making Endowment Gifts

Part of identifying the right prospects involves knowing what might motivate persons to establish an endowed fund. As you meet with and continue the cultivation of endowment gift prospects, keep analyzing what drives them to give. Knowing this will help you successfully close more gifts.

Donor needs may include:

* Honoring/memorializing loved ones or one's self.

* A sense of duty.

* Achieving a level of status and/or recognition.

* Alleviating guilt.

* Desire to belong or be more fully accepted.

* Intention of passing on personal values/beliefs.

Encourage Employees To Establish a Naming Gift

In addition to encouraging your organization's employees to consider a naming gift, why not give them the option of making a collective gift (as a department or an entire body) to establish a naming gift in honor of someone they jointly respect: a retired employee, a famous person.

MARKETING PLANNED GIFTS AS A WAY TO BUILD ENDOWMENT

Some people established named endowment funds during their lifetimes. Others choose to establish such funds after their lifetimes. And some choose to establish endowment funds while they are alive and then add to them after their lifetimes.

Deferred Gift Annuity May Appeal to Major Donors

A deferred gift annuity is a contract between a donor and an organization in which the donor makes a gift of cash or marketable securities and the organization promises to pay the donor fixed annuity payments beginning on the date the donor requests until the end of the donor's life. Most organizations require a minimum contribution of $10,000 to set up a deferred gift annuity. The agreement is irrevocable.

Donors must wait at least a year after establishing a deferred gift annuity before receiving annuity payments. The longer payments are deferred, the higher the rate that is applied, and thus the larger payments the donor receives. Payments begin on the date dictated by the donor when he/she sets up the gift. Payments are a fixed percentage of the original contribution amount and organizations usually have stated annuity payment dates. These are usually semi-annual or quarterly, but could legally be monthly or annually.

The donor qualifies for a tax deduction at the time the gift is made, which is a function of market value of the gift, age of beneficiary(s) (maximum of two), IRS discount rate and length of time of the deferral. Part of the annuity payment may also be received as tax-free income for a period of years tied to the annuitant's life expectancy.

Some donors create deferred gift annuities each year leading up to a specific year when they want to start receiving the annuity payments, for example, at retirement.

Planned giving consultant Debra Ashton, president, Debra Ashton Associates (Quincy, MA) and author of "The Complete Guide to Planned Giving: Everything You Need to Know to Compete Successfully for Major Gifts, 3rd edition," says donors who would set up a deferred gift annuity are interested in receiving an income from a gift today, but don't need the income immediately.

"A good prospect for a deferred gift annuity needs a large tax deduction now, but wants to set up a vehicle for retirement," Ashton says.

Ashton says a good prospect for a deferred gift annuity would meet these criteria:

❑ Wants to provide for a spouse or loved one at a future date.

❑ Doesn't have enough money to fund a Charitable Remainder Trust, which generally takes $250,000 for it to be viable.

❑ Could donate $5,000 or $10,000 per year over several years to set up a staggered income plan.

❑ Has highly appreciated securities and wants to convert them to a future income stream without paying the full up-front capital gain tax from a sale on his/her own.

❑ Wants to support a charity but cannot afford to give up the income.

❑ Has certificates of deposit coming due and wants to secure a generous fixed future income as well as make a charitable gift.

Sources: Debra Ashton, President, Debra Ashton Associates, Quincy, MA. Phone (617) 472-9316. E-mail: debralashton@comcast.net

> *Deferred gift annuities serve as one viable option to offer donors as a way to build your organization's endowment.*

Publicize Bequests To Receive More of Them

Publicizing the generosity of those who have made bequests will encourage others to consider similar acts of magnanimity. To make known how others have remembered your charity with a bequest:

1. Purchase and place in a prominent spot in your facility a specially designed wall hanging bearing names of those who have remembered your charity in their wills.

2. Tie undesignated bequests to a particular capital improvement or endowed fund and name it in honor of the donor.

3. Make mention of realized bequests in your publications and derive as much publicity as possible through media outlets.

4. Host an open house or reception once a bequest has been used to make an improvement or, if used for endowment, is beginning to make an impact.

If the donor has family, extend gratitude to them and keep them informed of how the donor's generosity is being recognized, add them to your mailing list and take other steps to embrace them as members of your charity's family.

Maintain Connections With Bequest Donors' Families

"Do you involve scholarship recipients of older endowments (those with no living or known donor contacts) in stewardship activities, such as writing thank-you notes to donors, and attending your annual scholarship luncheon? If so, how?"

"Oftentimes we will use the students who are attached to endowed funds that no longer have a living donor to help us with our stewardship of donors who have expressed an intent to establish a scholarship through a bequest. This way all scholarship students are able to be involved and we can steward our bequest donors even though they do not yet have a student attached to their scholarship."

— *Laura Yeager, Stewardship Manager, Culver Academies (Culver, IN)*

"We always invite the student recipients of memorial scholarships to our annual scholarship event, even if there is no living donor contact. We then ask either the associate dean or the program head from the students' area of studies to present the scholarship on behalf of the family. We also give each student a brief bio about the person memorialized."

— *Susan Walters, Awards Coordinator, BCIT Foundation (Burnaby, British Columbia, Canada)*

"If we receive acknowledgment letters for an endowment with no contact, we try to send them to members of our planned giving society who decided to establish a scholarship after they pass. Doing this is good stewardship. It means that the letters are not wasted, and it's a nice touch for those individuals who will not see their gift in action during their lifetime."

— *Robin Banker, Assistant Director of Donor Relations, North Carolina State University (Raleigh, NC)*

"We do not ask students receiving scholarships for which we have no living contact persons to write letters or participate in our scholarship luncheon (we don't have room for all the students whose donors might choose to attend). However, we do invite people who have arranged to fund a scholarship through a planned gift to attend the luncheon, and we try to seat them with students with whom they may have common interests. They will never see the recipients of their scholarships, but they really enjoy the chance to meet current students."

— *Marcia Casais, Assistant Director, Advancement Communications, Drew University (Madison, NJ)*

Invite scholarship recipients to write thank-you letters or attend your annual scholarship luncheon as a way to steward donors.

Convince Board Members to Make Planned Gifts

It's worth the effort to convince board members to make planned endowment gifts to your organization.

Why? For several reasons, including: 1) If board members aren't sold on the value of planned gifts to your organization, how can they expect others to make such gifts? 2) Likewise, board members who have made planned gift provisions will be much better equipped to sell others on the idea; and 3) board members — more than any other constituency — should realize the tremendous good that can be accomplished through the realization of major planned gifts over time.

Here are some strategies you can use to convince your board members to make planned gifts:

The willingness of board members to step up to the plate with planned gifts (earmarked for endowment) will encourage others to do the same.

- Enlist the assistance of existing planned gift donors to help sell your board.

- Use regular meetings to educate board members on various aspects of planned gifts — types of gifts, ways in which they can be directed, naming opportunities, and so forth.

- If you have a planned gifts society, invite board members to help host its events.

- Use board meetings to recognize those having made planned gifts.

- Ask individual board members to help in identifying planned gift prospects.

- List the names of your board on all planned gifts materials — brochures, letterhead, newsletters, etc.

- Get your board to own and endorse your planned gifts policies and procedures.

The more your board members own your planned gifts program, the more likely they will become to set an example for others to follow.

MARKETING PLANNED GIFTS AS A WAY TO BUILD ENDOWMENT

Earmark Unrestricted Bequest for Endowment-building Efforts

Does your organization occasionally receive a charitable bequest with no strings attached?

Although many nonprofits have a policy of earmarking such gifts toward their endowment, you might consider — one time — using such a gift for establishing or expanding your endowment program. Few efforts could be more important than investing resources into projects that generate even more revenue for needed programs and services.

Before your board haphazardly makes the decision to spend a bequest on current needs, much thought should be put into how those dollars should be earmarked. Remember, a bequest is the result of someone's entire life savings; it would be a travesty to unwisely use that gift for projects that produced unwanted results.

Develop a what-if plan to present to your board should they choose to designate one bequest toward your endowment efforts.

At right is an example of one scenario that a board might approve.

BEQUEST FUNDS DESIGNATED FOR RESTRICTED ENDOWMENT

If we receive a gift of:	*We will use it to establish/enhance our endowment fund in the following way(s):*
$25,000 or more	• Establish a named endowed scholarship fund.
$100,000 or more	• Establish an endowment to help underwrite a budgeted position.
$250,000 or more	• Endow the future maintenance of a new or existing building.
$500,000 or more	• Establish a named endowed fund to underwrite the costs associated with an existing program. • Establish a named endowed fund to underwrite the costs associated with a new program.

Gifts That Beget Gifts

Gift Opportunity —

Establish a planned gifts stewardship fund. Use annual interest from the fund to cover costs associated with the promotion, cultivation and stewardship of planned gifts, such as:

- Acquisition of a planned gift society plaque that displays names of planned gift donors in a public area of your facility.

- Underwriting the cost of an annual luncheon or dinner that recognizes and thanks all planned gift donors during their lifetime.

- Covering costs associated with the production of a regularly published planned gifts newsletter directed to a certain segment of your mailing list.

- Costs associated with running and managing your planned gifts advisory committee.

- Underwriting the cost of quarterly or annual estate planning seminars.

Solution —

Sell a prospect on the concept of establishing a stewardship endowment fund, annual interest from which would underwrite costs associated with promoting and stewarding planned gifts.

Donor Benefit —

Publicize in an ongoing way that your newsletter, recognition banquet or seminar is made possible through the [Name of Donor] Stewardship Fund.

In addition, the donor has the satisfaction that his/her gift is one which will serve as a catalyst in helping to generate planned gifts for a worthy cause.

Endowment Builder: Practical Ideas for Securing Endowment Gifts, Second Edition.
Edited by Scott C. Stevenson.
© 2009 Stevenson, Inc. Published 2009 by Stevenson, Inc.

WAYS TO RECOGNIZE AND STEWARD ENDOWMENT DONORS

Unlike a one-time gift for a capital improvement or a piece of equipment, named endowment funds carry with them greater donor ownership. Donors want to know about the health of the endowment. They want to know what their funds are doing on a year-to-year basis.

Steward Those Who Have Established Endowed Gifts

Do you provide a formal yearly update to persons who have established endowed funds with your organization? Informing these donors of their fund's status and impact should be a must for two reasons: It's a good stewardship practice and doing so could very easily lead to donors adding more to established funds.

Make a point to formally update your endowment donors annually as to their fund's status. Those ongoing acts of stewardship may result in additional gifts.

Meet one-on-one with those who have set up endowed funds to:

1. **Review the current progress over your organization's overall endowment for the past year.** Who is managing your endowment? Did the fund grow? At what rate? Were there any changes in your endowment's investment policy?

2. **Review the individual's established endowment fund.** What was the amount of annual interest used to underwrite the program for which the fund was established? What rate of return was made available and how was it calculated?

3. **How were the funds used?** If the endowed fund was a scholarship, for instance, who were the recipients and how much did each receive? Give the donor a solid sense of how the gift is having a positive impact on those you serve.

4. **Help the donor extend his/her understanding of the endowed fund to a higher level.** Paint a picture of what more could be accomplished were more funds added to the endowment, either through outright gifts, a planned gift or both. Do so in a way, however, that doesn't undercut what has already been contributed.

5. **Leave the donor with a written summary of your presentation.** Give him/her a document to review.

This formal update and stewardship procedure will make the donor more aware that his/her fund is a living gift that continues to impact your cause yearly.

Establish an Exclusive Club For Endowment Donors

Persons who make planned or annual gifts often have the opportunity to join giving clubs. Why not extend that opportunity to persons who make endowment gifts, too?

A club or society for persons who make an endowment gift at or above a set minimum both recognizes these important donors and motivates others to give.

Such a society might include:

❑ Members-only receptions or events throughout the year.

❑ Highly personalized tours of programs and facilities.

❑ An induction ceremony for new members.

❑ An endowment investment committee presentation on its growth and performance.

❑ A special listing in your annual honor roll of contributors.

❑ Invitations to periodic presentations that profile specific endowment funds and their impact on your organization and those you serve.

Host an Annual Event To Thank Endowment Donors

Just as you might host an annual event to thank all contributors at the $1,000-and-above level, consider hosting a similar event geared to the past year's endowment donors, assuming you have sufficient numbers to merit such an event. An endowment dinner or reception draws attention to the importance of building your endowment and also recognizes these important contributors.

You can use your event to:

• Point out endowment performance for the past year.

• Provide attendees with a printed handout that describes all named endowment funds and who supported each for the past year.

• Announce newly established endowment funds.

• Showcase the impact particular funds have on your nonprofit organization and the lives of those you serve.

• Generate publicity about your endowment by selectively inviting key media officials.

• Making special note of realized planned gifts for that year which have been earmarked for endowment purposes.

WAYS TO RECOGNIZE AND STEWARD ENDOWMENT DONORS

Elm Tree Society Thanks, Stewards Donors

Honor rolls, luncheons and gifts are just a few of the ways to thank and steward donors.

Staff with Scripps College (Claremont, CA) created a donor recognition society that uses those three methods and more. Currently some 300 members strong, the Elm Tree Society began in the early 1990s to honor and highlight planned giving donors and as a way for the college to show its appreciation to donors through elite events and gifts.

Allyson Simpson, director of planned giving, shares the details of the society:

What are the criteria to belong to the Elm Tree Society?

"A person must have made a life-income gift (e.g., charitable gift annuity, charitable remainder trust, etc.) or have communicated a testamentary bequest intention, including the designation of the college as the beneficiary of a life insurance policy, commercial annuity or a retirement plan, such as an IRA, 401(k) or 403(b) plan."

What does the college do with the society?

"We use the society to steward existing donors, thank and cultivate them for additional planned gifts. It has an aura of specialness about it, especially with respect to the appreciation gifts we give members, which usually bear the special society logo. This specialness also serves as an attraction for prospects we are cultivating as new planned giving donors."

What does the college do for members of the society?

"First, we feature the members prominently in the annual Honor Roll of Donors. Second, we hold at least two lunch/program events a year on campus and one or more lunch events off-campus where we have a critical mass geographically of members. Usually the president of the college welcomes and thanks those in attendance at the on-campus events. Third, once a year... we present all members with a recognition gift that identifies them as society members."

Why is this society successful?

"We engage in constant, year-round stewardship and appreciation. Our members come to anticipate the events and the gifts, and seem to really enjoy both and feel good about what they have done for the future of the college."

What challenges do you face with this society? How are you overcoming them?

"Planning and executing the events and staying in touch with members who live out of the area. Because the membership is predominantly elderly, sometimes our attendance is lower than we'd like. It's difficult for some of our more elderly constituents to get to campus or the event site. We try to schedule lunch events in conjunction with other programs on campus so there will be other persons coming to campus who might be able to drive the more elderly members who do not drive anymore. We also try to match people up geographically so they can come together.... When we send gifts to out-of-area members who can't make it to campus, we always send a warm letter thanking them again for their thoughtful gift and reminding them how important they are to the future of the college."

What advice do you have for organizations interested in creating a similar society?

- "Select a name that means something to the constituent body, since planned giving is all about legacy, emotional attachment and ultimate gifts. Our name comes from the Elm Tree Lawn on campus where every commencement is held. Just a picture of the lawn with its canopy of elm trees evokes memories and a sense of timelessness.

- "Publicize the society to existing planned giving donors and to likely planned giving prospects.

- "Steward, steward, steward on a consistent basis and show appreciation in important and visible, but relatively inexpensive, ways. We produce official membership certificates on a desktop computer that are signed by the college president. I try to choose recognition gifts that are useful for older persons (e.g., umbrella, luggage tag) and are inexpensive per unit, but still very classy, in the college's colors with the Elm Tree Society logo prominently displayed."

Source: Allyson Simpson, Director of Planned Giving, Scripps College, Claremont, CA.
Phone (909) 621-8400. E-mail: allyson.simpson@scrippscollege.edu

> Donor recognition societies are not only a great way to steward and honor donors, but to cultivate future donors.

WAYS TO RECOGNIZE AND STEWARD ENDOWMENT DONORS

What to Consider When Designing a Recognition Society

Designing a recognition society requires much more than coming up with a meaningful name and attractive benefits. "You'll also need to decide what you want to accomplish and what is manageable for your organization," says Judith T. Davis, marketing associate for gift planning, Virginia Tech (Blacksburg, VA).

Davis shares questions to discuss to help design a workable recognition society:

Make donor recognition a top priority. Put some time and thought into your donor recognition clubs or societies by answering these questions.

- How many members can our organization effectively recognize; how often?
- Will we recognize individuals only or include corporations?
- How will we handle joint gifts and household giving (including giving by unmarried couples in the same household)?
- How will we count gifts made by parent-members and credited to a son or daughter in order to gain membership for the son or daughter?
- How will we handle membership for spouses whose combined giving qualifies for membership, but who divorce, leaving one or both below necessary giving level?
- Will we count matching gifts?
- Will we count gifts in kind; at what value?
- Will we count pledges; how will we handle pledges that are not honored?
- How will we handle gifts for which there is a quid pro quo (e.g., season tickets)?
- Will we count deferred giving/estate gift commitments; how will they be valued?
- Will we require documentation for estate gift commitments?
- Will we need a separate deferred giving society; will members qualify regardless of gift value?
- What benefits of membership do we want to offer; how are these benefits meaningful to the donors; can the benefits be sustained?
- Will we do something special for charter members?
- Will we have a single-level giving society, tiered levels within one society, or multiple societies?
- Will we offer those nearing a tier threshold an opportunity to make an additional gift to advance to the next level? How will we notify them? Recognize them?
- What annual deadlines will be needed for new members to qualify in time to participate in an event or be listed on an honor roll?
- What staff member will be responsible for approving an offer of membership before it is made, and who will sign the offer letter?
- What will prompt a membership offer?
- How and when will we communicate with development officers about membership offers and advancements for their donors?
- When listing members, how will we balance consistent listing and donor preferences (e.g., will you use titles such as Dr. always, never, on request; use nicknames; list alumnus first; etc.)?
- How many levels of "anonymous" will we have (e.g., always; anonymous when gift ranges are mentioned; whenever specific amounts are mentioned; etc.)?
- How will we confirm donor preferences such as anonymity (e.g., a questionnaire with a limited menu of options; personal conversation; etc.)?
- How will we indicate membership, anonymity, induction date or other information on the database?
- How will we indicate on our database that a qualified person declined membership?

Source: Judith T. Davis, Marketing Associate for Gift Planning, University Development, Virginia Tech, Blacksburg, VA. Phone (540) 231-2279. E-mail: judithb@vt.edu

WAYS TO RECOGNIZE AND STEWARD ENDOWMENT DONORS

Design an Endowment Donors Display

A visible display of endowment donors' names can both encourage persons to give to endowment and recognize those who have already done so.

Whether it's a donor wall, kiosk or other display, showcase names of those who have made named endowment gifts (at a set minimum requirement) at a highly visible location on your premises (e.g., main lobby, reception area, lounge). Arrange names by year in which funds were established so names can be added in years to come.

Having an endowment-only donor display gives prominence to endowment gifts and encourages passersby to consider the possibility of establishing similar gifts.

Donation Stewardship Outlined in Policy

Donors, rest assured. The University of Notre Dame (Notre Dame, IN) leaves no question about donation stewardship. That's because for more than 12 years, the university has used a policy that defines its rules of conduct regarding the donations it receives.

Develop a policy that openly shares your commitment to endowment donors.

"Our obligation policy publicly shares our commitment to university donors," says Katherine Graham, senior director of development marketing, communications and stewardship. "They are more than guidelines; they are ethical statements regarding accountability."

The seven rules discuss issues such as acknowledgement, recognition, donation usage and impact reporting. The university shares its policy (shown below) online and in its annual stewardship report.

"We are blessed with loyal alumni, parents and friends who trust university leaders to use their gifts wisely and for the intention of the donor," Graham says. "Our Obligations of Stewardship confirm this mutual trust in writing."

When creating such a policy, Graham says to keep the list of guidelines short, use simple language and share the policy with as many audiences as possible.

Source: Katherine Graham, Senior Director of Development Marketing, Communications and Stewardship, University of Notre Dame, Department of Development, Notre Dame, IN. Phone (574) 631-9785. E-mail: katherine.graham@nd.edu

Development staff with the University of Notre Dame (Notre Dame, IN) follow this series of guidelines outlined in the university policy, "The Obligations of Stewardship:"

The Obligations of Stewardship, University of Notre Dame (Notre Dame, IN):

As a reminder of our obligation to effectively steward contributions made to Notre Dame, the university adheres to the following guidelines:

- All gifts should be acknowledged in a timely and personal manner.

- A contribution accepted with a restricted purpose must be used for that purpose.

- If the university finds itself unable to utilize a contribution for its stated purpose, this should be communicated to the donor so that an alternative usage can be arranged.

- Whenever feasible, and especially with endowment gifts, annual impact reports should be given to the donor.

- Proper recognition should always be given to the benefactor and public recognition must be approved by the donor.

- The value of any substantial benefits as a result of contributions must be reported to each contributor.

- Contributions will be accounted for using generally accepted accounting principles, which will provide a consistent, timely and accurate reporting of all gifts into the university's official financial record.

Thank you for your enduring support of the University of Notre Dame.

Recognizing Your Top Donor

 "What do you do to recognize your most significant donor in a significant way?"

"At the American Diabetes Association and with our Research Foundation, we have a standard set of recognition opportunities (personal tours during our scientific sessions, names in annual reports and ads in our consumer publication, Diabetes Forecast). But what makes our stewardship unique is that our stewardship director will discuss with our staff member and our donor ways that are meaningful to him or her. For example, we don't own a building, but we do have research grants that can be named in honor of the donor. Then each time the researcher is published, we give the donor copies of the article. We will also arrange personal lab tours at private gatherings for the donor and the scientists."

— *Elly Brtva, Managing Director of Individual Gifts, American Diabetes Association (Alexandria, VA)*

"This past year, the office of medical development raised several endowed professorships (each professorship is a $4 million gift). At a small dinner of about 50 people hosted by the dean of the medical school, we recognize the donor and the faculty who will be the chair holder. The donor and faculty member each receives a professorship medal and Stanford chair in addition to professionally designed photo albums commemorating the evening."

— *Lorraine Alexander, Senior Director of Development, Neuroscience Institute, Stanford University (Menlo Park, CA)*

"The Minneapolis Institute of Arts has a long-time trustee and major benefactor who has made countless gifts over his lifetime. During the opening of our new wing, we honored him and his legacy of support by announcing a permanent art endowment in his name. His fellow trustees had contributed nearly $4 million to this art endowment as a tribute to his decades of generosity.

"As a result, the museum — and the community — now have a permanent testament to this donor's commitment to excellence in our collections."

— *Joan Grathwol Olson, Director of Development, The Minneapolis Institute of Arts (Minneapolis, MN)*

Get Someone to Endow Recognition Events

Scenario — It's important to have an annual event for higher-end annual donors (e.g., $1,000-and-above). Doing so recognizes their generosity, while the event's exclusivity makes it more inviting for others to want to join this elite group.

Gift Opportunity — To underwrite the cost of an annual appreciation event or enhance an existing event, have someone endow this special affair. A $50,000 endowment, for example, would provide $2,500, based on a 5-percent return.

How it works — Annual interest from the fund could cover costs such as:

- Printing and mailing invitations.
- Printing a program that includes names of all higher-end donors from prior year. (If you print an overrun, give extras to prospective donors throughout the year, as well.)
- The cost of the meal.
- Decorations.
- A special keepsake for attendees.

Two possible donor benefits —

1. The donor could be publicly recognized and thanked each year as the one who has made the appreciation banquet possible. (This also has the benefit of a nonprofit justifying a lavish event since someone else paid for it.)
2. Donor gains satisfaction knowing his/her gift is playing an important role in attracting additional long-term support for your charity.

Sometimes budget constraints prevent us from providing the level of recognition that endowment donors deserve. To address that challenge, seek out a donor willing to underwrite donor recognition with an endowment gift.

WAYS TO RECOGNIZE AND STEWARD ENDOWMENT DONORS

Write Biographical Histories of Your Scholarship Donors

To help students write an appropriate thank-you letter to the person or family of the person who made their scholarship possible, Ellen Boehm, donor relations coordinator, Webster University (St. Louis, MO), writes brief biographical histories of each named scholarship.

Boehm places the biographical sketches in students' scholarship thank-you packets with a congratulatory cover letter, "Thank You 101" brochure, postage-paid return envelope and the program for Webster's annual scholarship luncheon.

"The biographical histories help students learn a little about the donor or foundation, giving them a personal connection with the folks behind the support," she says. Scholarships are in the program alphabetically, followed by pending scholarships (established but not fully endowed/ awarded), and future scholarships (deferred).

"We receive positive audience response to the history of the scholarships, and guests often take the program with them as a future reference," says Boehm. "Invited guests to the luncheon include all the donors of deferred gifts. We strategically seat these donors with students and other donors, giving them a feel for the future."

To continue cultivation and stewardship, she says, they send a copy of the program to the donors who were unable to attend the luncheon. The president also requests copies to hand to board members, and development officers request copies of the scholarship program to take with when visiting a prospective donor.

Source: Ellen Boehm, Donor Relations Coordinator, Webster University, St. Louis, MO. Phone (314) 968-5948. E-mail: boehmel@webster.edu

Here's an example of a biographical sketch of a named endowed scholarship fund that development officials give to students receiving the scholarship:

> ### The Margaret A. Fuhry Endowed Scholarship Fund for Graduate Students
>
> Margaret Fuhry's family established an endowed scholarship fund as a memorial tribute in 1997. An alumna of Webster University, Margaret Fuhry '77 was Director of Advancement Services at Webster at the time of her unexpected death. Margaret's memory is honored by her family through *The Margaret A. Fuhry Endowed Scholarship Fund for Graduate Students.*

Acknowledge Endowment Gifts With Thoroughness

Whenever an endowment gift is made, it's important to acknowledge the donor's investment thoroughly. A letter of thanks is not enough. The acknowledgment should include an update on status of named fund and general comments about your organization's endowment:

- How the fund's annual proceeds have been used during the past year.

- The impact of the fund on programs and/or services — how it is making a difference.

- The principle total within the donor's named endowed fund.

- The annual rate of return (interest rate and dollar amount).

- The total amount and health of your organization's endowment.

- A comment about the investment committee and its investment philosophy.

A thorough update on each endowment gift helps to keep the fund a living, viable gift that continues to fulfill its intended purpose and to motivate future gifts.

List All Endowment Funds In Honor Roll of Contributors

If you publish an annual honor roll of contributors for those on your mailing list, be sure to include a section that lists all endowment funds, even those to which no one contributed during that fiscal year. List the endowment fund in bold and those who contributed to that endowment fund immediately beneath it.

Those who contributed to a particular endowment will receive the recognition they deserve and endowment funds that received no contributions for that fiscal year will send a subtle message to make a contribution in the new fiscal year.

> Endowed Funds —
>
> Melissa and John Weinberg Endowment Fund
> • Melissa and John Weinberg
>
> Elston Macke Endowment Fund
>
> Robert Houston Endowment Fund
> • Sharon Houston
> • Martin Houston
> • Townsend Plumbing

WAYS TO RECOGNIZE AND STEWARD ENDOWMENT DONORS

Sample Challenge Report

Challenge Gift Update

Donor: **Estelle Radeker** Challenge Amount: **$2 million**

Matching Gifts Required: **$1 million** Stipulations: **None**

Pledge Date: **7/15/07** Challenge Duration: **24 months**

Start Date: **7/15/07** End Date: **7/15/09**

Challenge Restrictions:
Challenger's gift used to establish Radeker Endowment Fund; $500,000 in matching to be added to Radeker Endowment and $500,000 in matching to support general operations for five years ($100,000 per year beginning 7/1/06).

Update for Period **4/15/08**

Gifts of $10,000 or more —

Donor(s)	Pledge	Total New	Cumulative
Evenrude, Harker	$25,000		
Inness, Ian/Nancy	$50,000		
Kaplan, Susan	$30,000		
Klinger, Marty/Jill	$75,000		
Lineoff, Inc.	$100,000		
Morgan & Co.	$10,000		
Stravinski, Leon	$10,000		
		$300,000	$705,000

Gifts of Less Than $1,000 —

Previous Gifts	New Gifts	New Donors	Total Donors	
$240,000	$41,000	91	214	$281,000
			Total	**$986,000**

Keep Gift Challenger Informed of Matching Gifts

Let's say your organization finds a donor willing to put up a $2-million challenge gift if you can match it with an additional $1 million in gifts over a two-year period — a two-for-one match.

During that two-year period in which you are raising the $1 million, doesn't it make sense to keep the challenge donor up to date on your progress? Of course it does. That's why you should have an easy-to-read summary you can present to the donor on a quarterly basis. It keeps him/her closely involved as you are working to meet the challenge and also avoids any surprises throughout that time period.

Your report should include the challenge and matching amounts, duration of challenge (along with start and end dates), any restrictions, the names and amounts of significant gifts, stats of smaller gifts and cumulative matching gifts to date. Here's a sample design at left.

Share Your Endowment Expenditures Policy With Donors

Does everyone who has given to your endowment know how your organization calculates annual endowment expenditures? They should. Sharing the method used to determine annual endowment expenditures helps avoid possible misunderstandings.

Some nonprofits will make annual awards based on the endowment's overall earnings for the year. Others, meanwhile, may use a running average for a multi-year period to more accurately reflect the ups and downs of interest rates and equities performance.

Without any explanation of your rationale for annual endowment expenditures, some donors may think their endowment funds should be resulting in higher annual expenditures, while others may think you are unnecessarily dipping into the endowment's principle.

To avoid any confusion or misunderstandings, publish the formula your organization uses to determine how much endowment interest is used each year to fund particular programs/projects.

Sharing the method used to determine annual endowment expenditures helps avoid any potential misunderstandings. It's part of good stewardship protocol.

> Sample Endowment Disbursements Policy
>
> XYZ Charity makes quarterly endowment earnings distributions. Those distributions are determined by an eight-quarter trailing average of endowment earnings. Any average earnings in excess of 5 percent are returned to the endowment principle.

WAYS TO RECOGNIZE AND STEWARD ENDOWMENT DONORS

Donor Impact Reports Help Illustrate How Gifts Make a Positive Difference

Donor relations staff at The University of Kansas Hospital (Kansas City, KS) create donor impact reports as a tool to communicate to donors how their gift has made a positive difference to the area or program to which it was designated.

"Impact reports communicate our stewardship of their gift and keep donors engaged in future developments of the institution," says Andrea Villasi, program coordinator of donor relations for hospital fund development. "Frequent, personalized communication with your donors demonstrates the institution's and the fundraiser's responsibility to the donor. Communications like these strengthen the relationship with the donor."

Reports are customized to fit the size and scope of the gift and donor's personality, Villasi says. They are usually two to three pages long and include financial information, information on how the gift was used and plans for the remainder of the gift.

"Since our institution is a hospital, we also include stories about how our physicians, nurses and other staff have touched patients' lives," she says. "Adding color, photos and different fonts make the reports interesting and enticing to the donor."

While any level donor may receive a report, Villasi says, because the documents are so personal and detailed, they are usually reserved for major donors, those under cultivation or with whom the hospital has a special relationship.

Reports are generally sent one year after a gift is made, she says. "Any less than that and we might not have enough data to warrant a comprehensive report. Any more than 18 months might make a statement to the donor that we have forgotten about them, or that we aren't utilizing their gift as expected."

The number of reports donors receive depends on their relationship with the hospital, gift life span and if the donor has the capacity or intention to give again. Many donors receive an impact report once a year until the fund is depleted or

purpose of the gift has been fulfilled.

For organizations considering using donor impact reports as a stewardship tool, Villasi offers this advice:

"Know your donors and customize their reports to fit their personalities. If they are business savvy and are driven to give as an investment in their community, for example, the report should focus more on the financial outcomes of their gift. If the donor was compelled to give because

of an emotional experience, touching stories of how their gift has helped others will mean more to them than the amount of investment income that their gift has accrued in the last year."

Source: Andrea Villasi, Program Coordinator, Donor Relations, Hospital Fund Development, The University of Kansas Hospital, Westwood, KS. Phone (913) 588-1433. E-mail: avillasi@kumc.edu

This sample donor impact report illustrates how donor relations staff at The University of Kansas Hospital (Kansas City, KS) personalize information to specific donors.

Content not available in this edition

USEFUL ENDOWMENT REPORTS, FORMS AND POLICIES

The following pages include examples, samples and forms you will find useful as you market endowment gift opportunities and work to increase the size of your endowment.

Survey Helps Shape University's Endowment Fund Report

Stewardship officials with Florida Atlantic University (Boca Raton, FL) included a survey in their 2008 annual endowment report to provide an overall assessment of their report and find out how they could improve on it.

"Since my university is still very new to endowment reporting, we want to make every effort to ensure we are heading in the right direction," says Vanessa L. Diaz, coordinator of donor relations and stewardship. "Using the survey's feedback, we had an opportunity to adjust things to find a nice balance between providing too much and too little information."

Use your annual endowment report as an opportunity to seek input from donors.

The survey, sent to the university's endowment donors and shown here, asked questions such as if the report was easy to understand, if they wanted more or less information, and if they had ideas on how to improve the endowment report.

Based on feedback from the 2008 survey, Diaz and her co-workers changed the format of their endowment report for 2009. "The feedback on this year's report showed that donors responded more positively to the new layout," she says.

Other feedback from the survey led to adding a category for state-matched funds or additional gifts that came in during the fiscal year, combining several funds into one report (if the donor has multiple endowments), and providing a multiple-year summary.

Below is a portion of the survey used by stewardship officials with Florida Atlantic University to assess their annual endowment report.

Content not available in this edition

"For future reports, we will also be taking into consideration that many of our donors have had endowments for up to 41 years and the idea of showing the progression of their endowment over the years," says Diaz.

Overall, she says, they found the feedback from the first survey very helpful and will most likely send a survey again this year. "The questions we ask will be similar to last year's survey, but may be more specific," she says. "Our goal is to provide each of our donors with a concise and informative summary of their fund."

Source: Vanessa L. Diaz, Coordinator of Donor Relations and Stewardship, Florida Atlantic University, University Advancement, Boca Raton, FL.
Phone (561) 297-0058.
E-mail: Vanessa.diaz@fau.edu

USEFUL ENDOWMENT REPORTS, FORMS AND POLICIES

Endowment Agreement Spells Out Expectations

What sort of agreement form do you use for donors who establish endowment funds at your charity?

An endowment agreement is a legal agreement between a donor and an organization. According to Portland State University Foundation's (Portland, OR) Policy and Procedure Guide, the endowment agreement states the donor's intended restrictions and the purpose of the fund. "It ensures we are following the donor's intent," says Lisa Cox, gift processing coordinator.

The PSU Foundation developed its endowment agreement form two years ago with the help of its legal counsel. An attached memorandum of understanding outlines scholarship or faculty award guidelines. The endowment language should be as broad as possible to ensure future flexibility.

When PSU has a donor who wishes to establish an endowment fund, a development officer first reviews the endowment agreement form with the donor. After the fund's name, purpose and wording are decided, foundation staff create the document. It goes through a series of signatures, including the executive director, donor, president's office and back to the foundation office. Cox then opens two accounts: payout and corpus. Payout holds the portion of market earnings available for expenditure and donations made to the corpus must remain unspent in perpetuity unless released by the donors in writing. The Policy and Procedure Guide states the minimum amount needed to establish and name an endowment is $20,000 and interest will not be earned on gifts received before the $20,000 minimum balance is raised. The fund will be entered into the investment pool and will begin earning interest once the $20,000 is received.

Cox says the most complex issue when dealing with endowment agreements is making changes to the agreement when the donor is deceased. This prompted the insertion of an alternate use clause in the endowment form referenced in section three of the endowment agreement (see illustration).

For more information, visit http://foundation.pdx.edu/fs/default.jsp.

Source: Lisa Cox, Gift Processing Coordinator, PSU Foundation, Portland State University, Portland, OR. Phone (503) 725-5079. E-mail: lisacox@pdx.edu

Content not available in this edition

USEFUL ENDOWMENT REPORTS, FORMS AND POLICIES

Produce User-friendly, Professional Pledge Reminders

Donors who have made significant pledges deserve more than the usual pledge payment coupons that are often sent to those pledging at more modest levels.

If you're not able to deliver a pledge reminder in person, provide donors with a personalized reminder that clearly documents the pledge amount, amount paid to date, payment schedule and pledge balance. Spelling out the status of a current pledge helps to avoid misunderstandings on either side.

Equally important, include any updates that speak to the gift's impact to date. How is the gift furthering your organization? How is it positively impacting those served by your institution or agency?

The business of making the next pledge payment will be a much more joyful experience if your message conveys the positive impact of that gift.

Develop a template, such as the example shown here, that can be tailored to each donor who has an approaching pledge payment deadline, and send it about 45 days in advance of the due date.

A simple but friendly pledge reminder can be very effective in getting pledges paid by payment deadline. In fact, pledge reminders can be considered an act of stewardship if shared in a personalized and respectful way.

Sample pledge reminder for a major gift.

BOYS AND GIRLS CENTER

June 2, 2009

Dear Russ and Sharon:

As requested, I'm sending you this friendly reminder regarding the next (third) payment on your $100,000 pledge. According to the pledge you established in 2007, the next payment of $20,000 should be made on or around July 1. I have enclosed a return envelope for your convenience.

Although your named endowment gift has yet to be fully funded, your prior contributions are already having a tremendous impact. Thanks to the Russ and Sharon Eldridge Summer Camp Endowment, 13 students are attending this year's camp who otherwise would not be able to afford it. I've enclosed a brief summary of each of these children so you can learn a bit more about their backgrounds.

Thanks to your generosity, The Russ and Sharon Eldridge Summer Camp Endowment will continue to have a significant impact on the lives of young people for generations to come.

Thank you again for all you continue to do for The Boys and Girls Center.

Please don't hesitate to contact me if you have any questions regarding this next payment.

Sincerely,

Pamela Onst
Executive Director

The Russ and Sharon Eldridge Summer Camp Endowment	
Pledge: $100,000	Pledge Date: June 1, 2007
Annual Payments of $20,000	Beginning: July 1, 2007
Third Payment Due July 1, 2009	

USEFUL ENDOWMENT REPORTS, FORMS AND POLICIES

Create a Gift Acceptance Policy to Help Manage Gifts

A gift acceptance policy is a written document, reviewed periodically and accepted by a nonprofit's board, outlining how gifts are accepted from donors and under what terms, says Robert Evans, managing director, The EHL Consulting Group (Willow Grove, PA).

Such policies are especially helpful in accepting non-cash gifts, such as real estate, art and other items that appreciate in value, Evans says.

The policy should outline types of gifts a nonprofit will or will not accept and how those types of gifts are handled so that as either donors or staff discuss gifts, they don't make a misstep.

Crafting such a policy is also a great opportunity for discussion at the board level, he says, to help educate these key players about types of gifts accepted.

"Especially as you contemplate going into a campaign, it's important to either create a gift acceptance policy or review your existing one," he says. The policy should be relevant for all gifts and in sync with current IRS valuation guidelines.

Policies that address various contingencies help representatives appear knowledgeable and willing to accept the generosity of potential donors, says Evans. Without such a policy, "you may be presented with an inappropriate gift or one with so many strings attached that it will create a problem between the donor and recipient."

Source: Robert Evans, Managing Director, The EHL Consulting Group, Willow Grove, PA. Phone (215) 830-0304. E-mail: revans@ehlconsulting.com

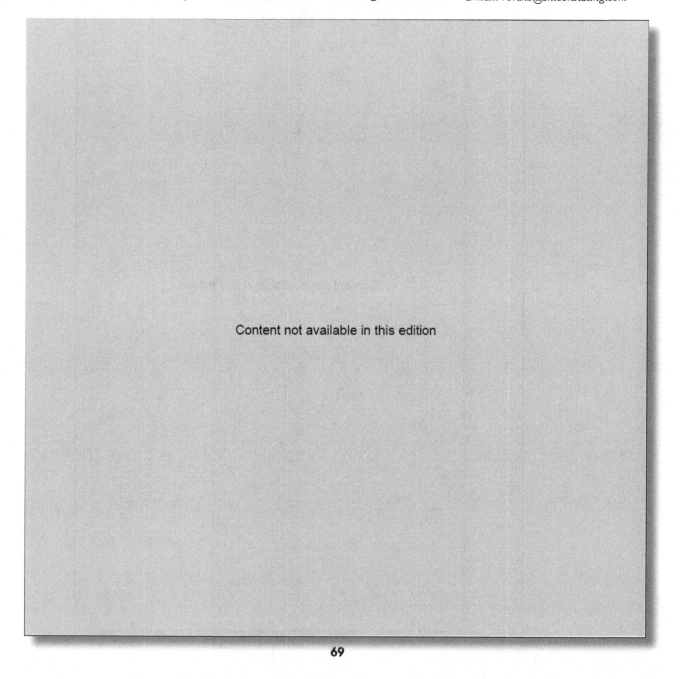

Content not available in this edition

USEFUL ENDOWMENT REPORTS, FORMS AND POLICIES

Endowment Policies Need a Code of Ethics

If you don't already have such a policy, a code of endowment ethics helps to set the highest of standards.

It's important today more than ever to maintain a code of ethics as a key element of your endowment investment policy.

As the late internationally recognized philanthropic consultant Arthur Frantzreb pointed out: "Confidence in America's nonprofit sector will, without question, impact the level of philanthropy experienced by organizations throughout the nation."

Frantzreb stressed the importance of sharing endowment investment policies and procedures in a very open way with constituents. He pointed out that simply sharing endowment income with constituents is not enough.

Frantzreb encouraged all nonprofits to develop and adhere to a code of ethics for endowed investment policies as an invaluable means of maintaining the highest of possible standards. Below he shared this draft as a catalyst to further such change.

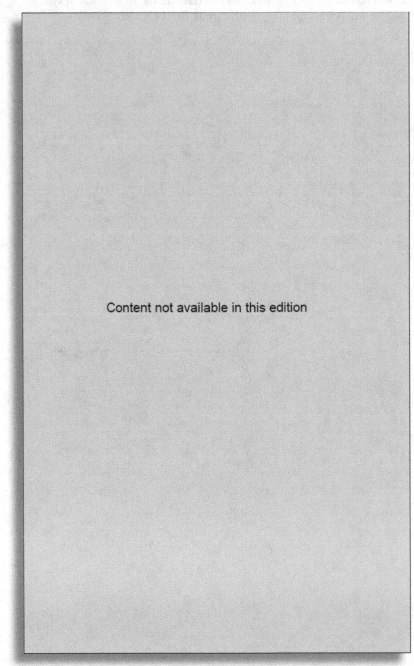

Content not available in this edition